WHAT OTHERS SAY ABOUT JEANETTE FRUEN

Jeanette (Fruen) Turk has emerged as the canny leader of a new breed of political strategists.

—THE WALL STREET JOURNAL
Front-page Profile

Jeanette Fruen is a rare natural resource, a rock of experience and persistence who has won countless impossible fights against entrenched interests. Don't get angry—get this book and win!

—GAIL SHEEHY
Author of *Passages, The Silent Passage*

I've worked with Jeanette Fruen on pro-choice campaigns and the "Packwood matter." Her successes on those toughest of issues prove she's among the best political strategists in the nation.

—GLORIA STEINEM

Jeanette Fruen's work on the Packwood case proves that people can make a difference.

—EDWIN H. ARMSTRONG, Co-Chair
Oregonians for Ethical Representation
Chief of Staff to three Republican governors

When others became discouraged, Jeanette Fruen just thought up new strategies. Her persistence and organizing skills played a key role in winning the long struggle for justice for the victims of Senator Bob Packwood.

—HARRIETT WOODS, Past President
National Women's Political Caucus

Jeanette Fruen's political strategies, grassroots organizing abilities, fund-raising expertise, media relations skills, and three years of tenacity were invaluable in bringing the Packwood case to its just end.

—BETTY ROBERTS
Women's Legal Advocacy Fund
Former Justice, Oregon Supreme Court

Jeanette demonstrated incredible energy, sound judgment, and an unswerving commitment to excellence (when we worked together in Orange County, California).

—LES FRANCIS
Legislative Projects Coordinator
The White House

Jeanette's years of experience managing tough campaigns has given her a command of the full range of tools available in today's political arena.

—DAVID MITCHELL, Partner, GMMA
Washington, D.C.
Consultants, Clinton/Gore Campaign

Jeanette has a positive attitude, an enthusiastic and dynamic personality.

—JOAN RICH, President
League of Women Voters of California

She is a winner.

—CECIL L. ALEXANDER
Vice President
Public Affairs
Arkansas Power & Light

Her poise and ability to speak effectively in such circumstances (making public statements) was outstanding.

—JOAN S. PETTY, President
League of Women Voters
Orange County, CA

Jeanette Fruen's skills, creativity, commitment, and determination, used in the context of a political struggle which might easily have never been resolved, were essential to the startlingly positive conclusion. Many people are indebted to her.

—MARY HEFFERNAN
One of "The Courageous Women"

Jeanette Fruen knew in her heart from the beginning that we would win.

—MARY NOLAN, Co-Chair
Oregonians fro Ethical Representation
Founder/Past President, Oregon NARAL

Even in the face of powerful opposition, (her) tireless efforts mobilized the pro-choice majority in Washington state. This is a victory not only for the state of Washington, but for women across America.

> —FAYE WATTLETON, President
> Planned Parenthood
> Federation of America

She adroitly balanced the effectiveness of paid advertising, especially TV, with personal grassroots communications.

> —MARY T. NOLAN, Past President
> Oregon NARAL

She had the orientation of a CEO. There were times when we resisted some of the cultural changes that she brought us. But that CEO orientation made a difference. She wasn't willing to feel any limitations.

> —JEANNE ATKINS, Public Affairs Director
> Planned Parenthood of the Columbia/Willamette

Her uncanny ability to assess the entire scope of a problem or potential problem, and effectively address the many facets of that problem, amazed even her most knowledgeable co-workers.

—Donald D. Adams
Government Consultant

Jeanette has a striking appearance and commands undivided attention when addressing a group.

—Diane Linn, Executive Director
Oregon NARAL

I have seen her skillfully unite warring factions and pull people together in a united front. I have seen her turn raw survey results into incisive, hard-hitting communications on topics as wide-ranging as nuclear power and a woman's right to choose.

—Ernest Paicopolos, Principal
Opinion Dynamics, Cambridge, MA

She has a great ability of thinking on her feet. And she put me at ease that she was open and ready to answer any question I thought important.

—Wayne Garcia
KIRO-TV News, Seattle

Jeanette Fruen helped our small group of Oregonians combat the cynicism and indifference of the national media and political insiders. I expect to use the strategies she created and the inspiration of her example in many future grassroots efforts.

—B. Carlton Grew
Attorney

**POWER
IN
THE
PEOPLE**

POWER IN THE PEOPLE

She Fought Sen. Packwood; Now She Outlines a Grassroots Workbook for Political Change in Your Neighborhood, State, and Nation

By Jeanette Lona Fruen

New Horizon Press   Far Hills, NJ

Copyright © 1996 by Jeanette Lona Fruen

All rights reserved. No part of this book may be reproduced or transmitted in any form whatsoever, including electronic, mechanical, or any information storage or retrieval, except as may be expressly permitted in the 1976 Copyright Act or in writing from the publisher.

Requests for permission should be addressed to:
New Horizon Press
P.O. Box 669
Far Hills, NJ 07931

Fruen, Jeanette Lona
    Power in the People: She Fought Sen. Packwood; Now She Outlines a Grassroots Workbook for Political Change in Your Neighborhood, State, and Nation.

Library of Congress Catalog Card Number: Pending

ISBN: 0-88282-142-3

New Horizon Press

Manufactured in the U.S.A.

2000 1999 1998 1997 1996 / 5 4 3 2 1

To my daughters,
Carrie and Christine,
with much love and great admiration.

CONTENTS

Acknowledgments—The Genesis of this Book ix

PART I:
ORGANIZING FOR ACTION—Seven Steps to Success 1
1. Swinging into Action with An Effective Action Committee 5
2. Assessing the Committee's Resources 21
3. Fund-Raising 27
4. Public Disclosure, Finance Reports, and Tax Status 55
5. Getting All the Facts 59
6. Polling 63
7. Making a Plan for Action 73

PART II:
BUILDING PUBLIC SUPPORT—Putting Your Action Plan to Work 81
8. Communicating Persuasive Messages 83
9. Getting Editorial Support 109
10. Letters to the Editor 113
11. Speaking Opportunities 117

PART III
GETTING ACTION—Turning Goals Into Reality 131
12. Lobbying 133
13. Testifying at Public Hearings 145
14. Observing and Monitoring 151
15. Working on the Inside 159
16. Supporting Supportive Public Officials 163
17. Electing Supportive Officials 169
18. Using the Legal System 173

PART IV:
THE BALLOT MEASURE—When All Else Fails 177
19. The Ballot Measure 181

PART V:
PEOPLE-POWER SUCCESSES—And How These People Won 195
20. People-Power Successes 197

PART VI:
CONCLUSION 211

ACKNOWLEDGMENTS

The Genesis of This Book

"Jeanette, you'll never guess what I just did."

"Gee, David, since we haven't talked for nine months, I can't imagine."

"I got authorization to write a front-page profile of you in The Wall Street Journal."

It was that telephone conversation with David Shribman, then staff reporter for *WSJ* and now Washington, D.C., bureau chief for *The Boston Globe* and winner of a Pulitzer Prize in 1995, that began my adventure as an author. After the profile appeared in November 1991, New York City-based literary agents, Ling Lucas and Ed Vesnesky, called and asked if I'd write a book. They walked me step by step through the proposal process and were pleased with the results but couldn't sell it.

A year later, I became obsessed with working on behalf of a small team of Oregonians in support of the women who came forward to tell their stories about Bob Packwood's acts of sexual misconduct against them. The book proposal was set aside until another phone call.

This one was from Jennifer Lauck, a publicist in Portland, Oregon, who was working with Ling on another project. Ling suggested that Jennifer call me. They had agreed that if I got on a speaking tour, that would help build credibility for me and entice a publisher to take on *Power IN the People*. Jennifer and I met, she read the proposal and said she'd like to try to sell it. Like so many of the self-confident dreamers in my life, so "knew" she could "Just do it!"

POWER IN THE PEOPLE

She was right! Within weeks New Horizon Press bought the book and I had an Author's Contract and an advance on the basis of the proposal and one chapter.

As you read the book you'll meet some of the most important people in my professional life and some personal friends. There are too many others to mention individually—my life runneth over with wonderful, supportive friends with whom I've shared amazing experiences. To each of these people whose magic has touched my life, my most grateful thanks!

PART I

ORGANIZING FOR ACTION
Seven Steps to Success

Poster:

Someday we will all be free.

**That Day Has Come
Please Vote.**

Archbishop Desmond Tutu,
Johannesburg, South Africa

Since 1989, political power has surged in people around the world. Common people with common dreams tore down the Berlin Wall. Blacks caused the end of the uncivilized and unjust apartheid monster in South Africa. Russian mothers with bouquets of flowers stopped tank-driving invading soldiers. And the bold, heroic students at Tianamen Square have only temporarily lost their fight for freedom in China. History teaches that "the wrong shall fail, the right prevail."

Meanwhile Americans, feeling less and less confidence in our political system, have begun to make our dissatisfactions

POWER IN THE PEOPLE

known. With dynamic action we're changing our government in ways not seen since the civil rights and anti-war movements three decades ago. We're using our people power.

- In 1995, a small, tenacious team of Oregonians was instrumental in Bob Packwood's unprecedented exit from the United States Senate.
- In 1994 Americans, disenchanted with politicians fiddling while critical national issues went unattended, put Republicans in control of Congress for the first time since the mid-fifties.
- In 1992, Americans volunteered and contributed in record numbers to political campaigns across the nation, including that of a third-party candidate for President, Ross Perot. Perot gained 18 percent of the popular vote, and there was a short period of reenergizing spirit in 1992, which continued into the election of Bill Clinton. Very soon thereafter, however, the climate of disenchantment returned.

What caused this disenchantment? The answers are many and complex. One inadequately noted cause is Americans' mistaken expectation that when we vote, our government will work in the ways we want it to.

How can we revitalize our government? By understanding that it takes more than an occasional vote to make government respond to the will of the majority. It takes patience, discipline, hard work, courage and expertise. Many Americans have all these but the expertise.

By sharing the lessons I've learned over four decades of political activism, I hope you'll gain the expertise and confidence to make our precious democracy work better. Responding to widespread complaints about "special interest groups" and professional lobbyists, I hope *Power IN the People* will serve as the manual for the biggest "interest group" of all: you, the American people, advancing your interests in communities across the nation.

ORGANIZING FOR ACTION

This hands-on workbook:
- Gives the tools you need to organize for successful political action, build public support for your cause, and, thereby, create the political climate necessary to force political leaders into responsive, responsible action;
- Shows how to create the political climate necessary to push elected and appointed officials into creative, problem-solving action;
- Provides a step-by-step guide on how to use the most current and effective grassroots techniques;
- Demonstrates that the elements of effective citizen participation can be used at all levels of government: to get a stop sign to protect pedestrians approved by a City Council; to adopt a state-wide health plan; or to get a United States Senator to resign after allegations of sexual misconduct are disclosed;
- Tells you how to win ballot measure elections.

    I offer you the non-partisan, universally applicable methods and sound practical "insiders" advice "special interest groups" buy for millions of dollars every year—but from my perspective, which includes the experience of working from the ground up.

    We Americans must use our power to move into the next millennium with confidence in our democratic process and the knowledge and commitment to make it better. There can be no greater tribute to the wise visionaries who wrote our Constitution in 1776, the freedom fighters who defeated the British in 1781, the African-Americans and women who forced amendments guaranteeing the right to vote to all citizens, and the hero and heroine protectors of freedom abroad and our rights at home. There will be no greater heritage to the generations that follow us.

    Here's to Power **IN** the People!

1

SWINGING INTO ACTION WITH AN EFFECTIVE ACTION COMMITTEE

Democracy is the worst form of government except all other forms that have been tried from time to time.

Winston Churchill

Imagine we're having coffee in your living room, sharing new-friend talk. The weather. Our families. When I say I'm a political consultant, you tell me you want to get involved in politics—there are things happening in your community you don't like—but you don't know where to start.

I ask you:

Are you ready to use your power?

Is this issue your pet peeve—or are there a lot of people in your community who are bothered by it, too?

Are you willing to spend time, money, energy—and do you have the heart and the patience—to solve this problem?

I remind you of one of the most consistent rules of life: Everything always takes more time, money, and energy than we expect.

POWER IN THE PEOPLE

You answer YES to all these questions, but you're hesitant when I ask if you're willing to lead the effort. You've never been a leader in anything. You see yourself as shy, terrified of public speaking, lacking in confidence, with no political experience.

The person you describe was me in the mid-nineteen sixties. But have courage! I've written this book based on the experiences that transformed my timid soul into one which resides in the person *The Wall Street Journal* called the "canny leader of a new breed of political strategists;" one who knows from her own experience that we each have many, untapped talents—and we each can make a difference!

So let's begin.

Defining Your Goals

First, you need to describe the issue you want to work on so people you talk with know exactly what you want to accomplish—and so you have an achievable goal.

Definitions That Are Too Broad	Definitions That Are Clear, Brief, Specific
Safe streets	Install a stop sign on my corner
Better education	Improve reading test scores
The city is getting too crowded	Adopt a long-range growth plan
Too many people can't afford health insurance	Adopt a state-wide health plan
Ethical representation in the government	Get the senator guilty of sexual misconduct out of the Senate

SWINGING INTO ACTION

Now clearly define your goal so that you communicate exactly what you want to accomplish:

_____
_____
_____

Finding the Target

Next, you need to figure out which governmental body handles the issue you're going to work on. There are many different government arrangements, but generally issues are handled as follows:

Issue	Government
Traffic and street safety	City, county
Education	School district
Growth and development of land	City council, county, state
Health care	County, state, federal
Conduct of elected federal officials	U.S. House of Representatives, U.S. Senate

To find out which government you'll be working with, call the League of Women Voters, a local newspaper, the reference library, and the local chamber of commerce. Tell the people you speak with what your issue is, your point of view on the issue, and ask who they suggest you talk with.

POWER IN THE PEOPLE

What governmental body is responsible for your issue?

Who should you talk with?

FORMING THE ACTION COMMITTEE

Now you're ready to start forming the Action Committee—the coalition of ten to fifteen individuals and leaders of organizations to help you lead the effort. I used to call this group a "coalition," but "Action Committee" is more reflective of the new sense of dynamic empowerment that Americans are expressing.

My wonderful friend and professional colleague, Rick Claussen, describes an Action Committee as "a room full of people who couldn't agree on another thing, but all agree that 'x' is good or bad." One of today's lead news stories gives a perfect example: the "unusual alliance" of the American Civil Liberties Union (ACLU) and gun-rights groups, including the National Rifle Association, joining forces to urge new controls to prevent abuse of power by federal law officers. "Unusual alliance" hardly describes this coalition!

And a great example *almost* came out of the "Packwood matter." Women's organizations—the National Women's Political Caucus, National Organization for Women, and Feminist Majority—were with us in the call for public hearings from the start of our efforts. The three most influential conservative Christian groups added their voices for public hearings in May 1995. What a news conference: the presidents of the three women's groups—fem-Nazis, some call them—and the leaders of the three leading Christian groups all calling for public hearings! It was only in my dreams.

SWINGING INTO ACTION

Why is an Action Committee important?

1. A broad-based group working together—sharing resources of people, money, talents, and diverse opinions—is more powerful and influential than an individual or single organization working alone.
2. The ability to develop and implement a coordinated strategy is greatly enhanced.
3. Resources are maximized by minimizing energy, time, and money spent in organization and management.
4. Communications with the public-policy making body you're trying to influence are focused and strategically timed.
5. Opportunities for error in reporting of contributions and expenditures are minimized.

What does an Action Committee do?

An Action Committee creates political pressure and builds momentum forcing change. To force this change, an Action Committee develops and implements a plan, and coordinates all Committee activities including fund-raising, polling, speakers bureau, writing letters to the editor, getting editorial support, lobbying, testifying, monitoring, seeking appointments to key positions, getting people with similar points of view elected, and using the legal system. The Committee does the actual work or directs hired staff. (The Committee spokesperson is not necessarily an active member of the Action Committee. See Chapter Six.)

Why is it important to build a broad-based Action Committee?

The more representative of the community's diversity, the greater the influence and potential for success. Imagine yourself

POWER IN THE PEOPLE

as a school board member. The subject on the school board's agenda is a reading curriculum. Would you be more persuaded by a presentation of one teacher or a presentation by an ethnically diverse group including students, men and women, teachers, parents, business leaders, and senior citizens?

As you build the Action Committee think: *men and women, diversity, inclusion.*

It isn't necessary for Committee members to know or like each other or even to think alike—they just have to agree to work together for a single, common mission.

Where do you look for potential members of a broad-based Action Committee?

Lots of places.
- Committee members' families, friends, neighbors, business contacts.
- Many chambers of commerce have a list of local organizations available for community use.
- "Let your fingers do the walking" through the Yellow Pages Index.

Here's a sample of organizations you might consider:
- Professional organizations (physicians, architects, attorneys, nurses, bankers, engineers).
- Trade/business associations (chambers of commerce, labor unions, farmers, contractors, realtors).
- Environmental/sports (Audubon, Sierra Club, Ducks Unlimited, Wildlife Federation).
- Ethnic (League of United Latin American Citizens [LULAC], National Association for the Advancement of Colored People [NAACP], Urban League, Rainbow Coalition).
- Education (teachers' association, school board, school

SWINGING INTO ACTION

administrators, college professors, PTA).
- Civic (American Association of University Women [AAUW], American Association of Retired Persons [AARP], Business and Professional Women [BPW], Jaycees, Rotary, Kiwanis, League of Women Voters, League of Cities, mayors' conference, neighborhood associations).
- Churches and religious groups.
- Political parties and political action committees.

Look at your issue again and think of others who might have something to gain or lose by the issue. Are there any potential allies there?

Always keep your efforts non-partisan or at least equally bi-partisan. The letterhead of one committee, working to get legislation passed by a Republican-controlled state senate, listed eight elected Democrats in the top ten names. That's politically insensitive! Even the most politically naive person can figure out one reason the group didn't get its legislation passed. In many cases, it's unwise to include elected officials on your Committee. Politicians carry negatives: As a group, they're not highly regarded; some people have voted against them; their popularity may take big swings, depending on recent actions they've taken or not taken; they may have their own agendas. But they can be helpful in giving advice and counsel, fund-raising, and working inside the system.

Get people or organizations on your Committee who help define the issue for the media and the public. The co-chair of the committee working to get Republican Bob Packwood removed from the United States Senate because of his sexual misconduct was chief of staff to three Republican Oregon governors—so the media didn't describe it as a partisan issue. Early in the effort, twelve men called for Packwood's resignation at a news conference—so the media didn't define it as a woman's issue.

POWER IN THE PEOPLE

Get people on your Committee who will help make your issue become "the talk of the town." People listen to their friends, neighbors, co-workers on issues. During the Oregon pro-choice campaign, we moved up six percent in the polls before we did any public communications or advertising. That significant move happened simply because we had leaders of organizations on our Committee who put information about the issue in their monthly newsletters. They raised their members' awareness of the issue and the members started talking to other people.

When you're thinking about people for the Committee, remember a person's title is more persuasive and credible than that person's name. Which would be more convincing and trustworthy to you: "Betty Smith" or "Betty Smith, Retired Justice, State Supreme Court"? "Dick Jones" or "Dick Jones, President, Local Medical Association"?

Keeping these guidelines in mind, make a list of candidates for the Action Committee—the coalition of ten to fifteen individuals and leaders of organizations to help you lead the effort.

_____   _____
_____   _____
_____   _____
_____   _____
_____   _____

Now ask yourself: Is this list broad based? Is it reflective of the ethnic diversity of my community? Does it include men and women? Is it geographically balanced? If I didn't know anything about this issue, would I be more inclined to pay attention to it because of the credibility of the people and organizations on the list? As your Committee size increases, keep re-checking it against these criteria.

Once you've identified a prospect who might share your mission—even if for different reasons—have coffee or a phone

SWINGING INTO ACTION

conversation with the person or the organization's president to explore the possibility of working together. To build your confidence, start with people you already know. Talking with them will give you practice for talking with people you don't know. Tell them you're building an Action Committee to create political pressure and keep it focused on the right places until your mission is accomplished.

Then, when you have a group of six to eight individuals who agree to work with the Action Committee, invite them to your home or a convenient meeting place to talk about the issue. Have them recommend others to recruit to the Action Committee.

Is it important to have people sign something when they agree to join the Action Committee? Of course! Imagine how awkward it would be if—after stationery and materials are printed—someone announces that he or she hadn't joined the Committee. Here's a sample:

```
YES on #26-1 CAMPAIGN ENDORSEMENT CARD
You bet, I want to save our local greenspaces—trails, wildlife
habitats, recreational and forested areas—for future generations.
     That's why you may list me publicly as a member of the
                  YES on #26-1 Committee.
Signature_____
Name (please print)_____
Company/Organization*_____
Title*   _____
Address_____
City, State, Zip       _____
Phone, Daytime _____ Evening _____
          * Titles and affiliations for identification only.
```

When the card is returned to the Committee, you have an opportunity to send a follow up: "Thanks for joining . . . If you want to do more, please complete and return the enclosed card." It's a reason to be in their mailbox another time. Other managers prefer to include the options on the first card. Whichever way you

POWER IN THE PEOPLE

decide is most workable for your group, the options for volunteer support include: finance committee, speakers bureau, distributing materials, data entry, office support, etc.

ACTION COMMITTEE GROUND RULES

To prepare and help you feel confident for the first meeting of the Action Committee—which you'll facilitate—become familiar with the following material. You might even send copies to people before the meeting so at least a few of them will have given some thought to these ideas before the meeting.

How do you build a well-functioning Action Committee?

The Committee will want to adopt policies to build an effective, broad-based Action Committee, ensure a coordinated effort, protect the confidentiality of strategies and plans, and minimize the chance of error in reporting contributions and expenditures.

The following policies are probably more formal or complicated than your Committee needs—but they'll give you a place to start.

1. The policy making group—let's call it the Steering Committee—will have at least five members but no more than ten. Too few people leads to insular decision making; too many leads to rule by the most persistent person and causes decision making to be ineffective, time consuming, and cumbersome.

If you have a large coalition, you might consider the model I developed for the NO on 13 Campaign, the California ballot measure that began the national property tax revolt in 1978. The statewide coalition had over 125 organizations. Obviously, rapid, thoughtful decision making is impossible with that many participants. We solved the problem by creating five categories—business, organized labor, education, civic/volun-

SWINGING INTO ACTION

teers, and public employees. Three organizations from each category served on the Steering Committee. Representatives of those organizations were responsible for dialogue with other organizations in their category; distribution of materials was handled by the campaign staff. This process worked well for us and is an easily adaptable model for political issues even in non-election settings.

2. By joining the Action Committee, all people and organizations indicate their commitment to the mission, agree to actively participate, compromise, and support fund-raising, organizing, and campaign efforts. It's unproductive to have "hangers on" who want to set policy but don't have time, money or volunteers to commit to the cause. One statewide coalition on abortion rights required a $50,000 contribution before an organization could join its Steering Committee; another required the use of an organization's mailing list three times.

3. To create a climate where people from a wide range of backgrounds and political views will actively participate, only issues directly related to the Committee's mission will be discussed before, during, and after the meeting. You need everyone to feel comfortable enough to stay with the group.

4. To ensure the coordinated and consistent delivery of messages, only designated persons are authorized to make public statements on behalf of the Committee. This is the only assurance you have of keeping your message focused, consistent, and accurate.

5. All contributions will be made to and reported by the Committee. With many local and state governments requiring disclosure of funds and contributions received and spent by committees for lobbying efforts and campaign purposes, it's vital that funds be properly reported. You want to avoid making innocent mistakes that can undermine the credibility of your efforts or force you to make unnecessarily time consuming, expensive remedies for mistakes.

POWER IN THE PEOPLE

6. All participants agree to abide by the Committee's Confidentiality Policy. Such a policy is crucial when dealing with a very controversial issue. For example, having your survey results inadvertently released can have terrible consequences! Your opposition is alerted to your strategies. The results may be incorrectly reported—which means you'll waste time correcting the misinformation rather than discussing your issue. If the survey results are very good, people may decide you don't need money; if the results are bad, others won't give because they don't want to "support a sinking ship."

Here's the content for a Confidentiality Policy that could be adapted for your Committee's needs:

Confidentiality Policy

As a member of the (insert name), I am responsible to act in the best interest of the Committee, including protecting the confidentiality of information discussed at Committee meetings.

1. I agree, therefore, that I will protect all confidential information discussed during Committee meetings and will refrain from disclosing that information to any person, except those in my organization who need to know in order to make decisions regarding their level of support for the campaign. This confidential information includes survey results, strategies, messages, or any other information that could be useful to the opposition.

2. Each time new survey data is available or new strategies are developed, the Committee will determine if that information can be discussed publicly. Also, the Committee will provide language on how to characterize the information in discussions outside the Committee.

If I am unclear about what information should remain confidential, I will raise my questions with the Committee before revealing the information in question.

3. To ensure full and open discussion, all working meetings of the Steering Committee may be attended only by members of

SWINGING INTO ACTION

the Steering Committee and people working with the Committee, such as consultants. This rule keeps decision making simplest, meeting time productive, and protects confidentiality.

4. To ensure full and open discussion, all working meetings of the Steering Committee are closed to the media. When appropriate, a spokesperson will be available to the media immediately following such meetings.

5. All statements or materials for general public distribution must be coordinated with and approved by the Steering Committee before release of statements or production of materials. This is important for budget control.

At this point, there are two options: You decide which policies would be useful and/or adapt them to fit the Committee's needs, or you make copies of them for the group or a subcommittee of the group to discuss and work on. The first option may help the group get off to a faster start and can be revised by the group later; the second gives the group more ownership of the rules and is more democratic.

Preparing for the First Meeting

Now what do you do? Plan the agenda for the organizing meeting. If possible, mail or fax it out before the meeting. Members know what's coming, can ask questions, and can prepare for the meeting. It gives you the opportunity to call key people to ask if they want to add anything; you can also probe for problem areas.

Here's a sample agenda for a two-hour organizing meeting—which is the longest any grassroots meeting should be. At longer meetings, people will become unfocused, inattentive, undisciplined—they'll leave the meeting mentally or physically. I think it helps people make only new points and keep their com-

POWER IN THE PEOPLE

ments concise during discussion, to have a suggested time limit for each agenda item.

SAMPLE AGENDA

	Suggested Minutes
1. *Self-introductions*—names, reasons for interest in the issue, what he/she wants from the meeting;	10
2. *Discuss agenda points*; ask for other items that people want to add;	5
3. *Define the goal*—if people aren't comfortable with your definition, negotiate one;	10
4. *Discuss Action Committees*	10
a. What they do, why they're important, why it's important to build a broad-based Committee and how to do it.	
b. Brainstorm on how to build the coalition or recruit a subcommittee to bring suggestions to the next meeting;	10
c. As a way of helping people understand, review the Action Committee Creed:	5

ACTION COMMITTEE CREED

We've joined efforts with a single mission:
To (insert your group's goal).
We don't have to think alike, but we *must* work together.
No one of us is as good or influential as all of us.
There is more that binds us together on this issue
Than there is that separates us.

d. Endorsement Form—does the Committee like the form you've designed? If not, ask someone to bring an alternative to the next meeting;	10

SWINGING INTO ACTION

5. *Discuss the rules*, including a confidentiality policy, for building a well-functioning Committee. As a group, decide which ones are important for your group. Recruit a volunteer or subcommittee to bring options to the next meeting;   20

6. *Organize the Committee*—select a facilitator for meetings; a secretary to take minutes, send meeting reminders, prepare a roster for everyone; set a specific time for regular meetings;   10

7. *Have people say what they're responsible to bring to the next meeting;*   5

8. *Check to see that people's expectations of the meeting have been met;*   5

9. *Set goals for the next meeting;*   5

10. *Anything else people want to discuss;*   5

11. And, of course, *"pass the hat" for contributions.*   5

Empowered citizens take responsibility to base their opinions on fact; they take responsibility to clearly and briefly state those opinions, and they listen respectfully to the opinions of others.

Meetings should be based on:
1. Consensus, not governed by Roberts' Rules of Order;
2. Led by a team builder, *not* an egotist;
3. Directed by a facilitator, *not* a "boss."

Since people are leading such busy lives, it's important that the facilitator—with help from the group—always starts meetings on time and ends them on time. The facilitator—with help from the group—keeps the meetings on track. It's useful to have subcommittees for specific functions such as coalition building, writing coalition policies, and developing a fund-raising plan. With effective subcommittee work, Steering Committee

POWER IN THE PEOPLE

meetings will be so crisp that people know their time is well spent, they'll feel ownership of the project but not overwhelmed—and they'll stay on the team!

You've Made A Good Start!

Now take joy in what you've accomplished—you've started building to force political change in your community and you're growing personally in the process. This is just the beginning. Thank you for letting me help you find solid ground for political action and maybe learn how to fly. Let's keep working together so you'll soar with even greater confidence and skill.

And, yes, I'd like another cup of coffee, please.

2

ASSESSING THE COMMITTEE'S RESOURCES

Bumper sticker:

Democracy is not a spectator sport

No committee—unless its luckier than any I've worked on—can be successful without setting realistic goals based upon an *accurate* assessment of resources that will be available for the cause. This assessment must be made early in the organizing phase and will tell you what you can count on in terms of an individual's and organization's involvement and commitments of time, money, and volunteers.

In one instance, I didn't follow my own advice with sorry consequences. Early in a campaign, Nan Heim, a competent, professional colleague with whom I was co-consulting had one-on-one meetings with the leaders of the group that retained us. In these resource assessment meetings we were told one "angel" would contribute $100,000 and two others would give $50,000 each. We knew, too, that hundreds of others would make small

POWER IN THE PEOPLE

contributions because the issue—preserving greenspaces in the tri-County region of metropolitan Portland, Oregon—was so popular and its advocates had developed an extensive network. So we based the Campaign Plan and Budget on the premise that the campaign would raise about $250,000. Unfortunately, the assessments were not accurate. None of the three large contributions was received.

Had we known that less than $70,000 would be raised during the entire campaign, we certainly would not have spent $15,000 on a baseline survey!

To get a realistic picture of what will be available to you, you'll need to design a RESOURCE ASSESSMENT form. This form will guide your meetings with potential leaders and supporters of your effort. You must, of course, adapt the following questions to your own situation. And please learn from my mistake: Check and double check.

Whom to Ask

To stimulate your brainstorming, look at the list of potential members of the Action Committee. Remember, while some of the people on that list may not be effective Action Committee members, they may be a terrific source of other kinds of support. But ask each of them—Action Committee members and the others—for a one-on-one meeting to make your assessment of resources.

What to Ask

What organization and personal lists are available to you for this cause?

• Organizations have membership lists; individuals have their personal lists.

... THE COMMITTEE'S RESOURCES

- You'll need names; addresses, including zip codes; phone numbers; and donor history, if it's available.
- And, of course, in today's computer world it will be most efficient to receive the lists on a disk that's compatible with the computer your Committee will use.

What commitment for use of the lists can you count on?

If possible, get a commitment to use the lists three times during one year. This commitment is easiest to obtain when the months of normal fund-raising for the organization are different than the months you'd like to use the lists.

What commitment for contributions can you count on?

Can they help with start-up contributions? Are they members of organizations that have local, state, and national chapters? If yes, what help can you expect from them? How do you apply for contributions from them? Who should make the contact?

What Information can they provide to help you predict cash flow needs?

When can they make a contribution? When might any of the other sources of support they suggest make a contribution?

What in-kind contributions can they make?

This important support comes from people and organizations who can contribute money and other kinds of support or

POWER IN THE PEOPLE

who can give only other support. In-kind contributions include: loaned staff; office space and phone bank locations; office furniture, such as desks and file cabinets; equipment, such as telephones, computers and printers, fax and copier; office supplies, such as paper; services, such as printing, copying, and graphic design.

What commitment will volunteers make?

When I first began working in grassroots efforts three decades ago, many of us were full-time homemakers who got our adult contact through volunteer activities. We were the lifelines of grassroots politics. Even then, it was more difficult to get volunteers for issues—school bonds, land use—than for candidates.

So much has changed! My recent experience is that getting and keeping volunteers on issues is an extremely difficult task. Potential volunteers are most receptive if they are given a specific task with a specific time limit. High school and college interns, people in transition, and retirees all make competent, reliable, and delightful members of the team.

Successful volunteer relations are enhanced when volunteers know how important their work is and how it fits into the whole scheme of activities; they have specific goals; they know the results of their efforts; they are asked to work for a specific time.

Ask volunteers for input: What can we do better? What are we missing? And then use their suggestions as often as you can!

It's important, too, to validate volunteers' efforts and to thank them publicly on a regular basis! Without them, much needed work will not be done!

Here's a sample of a RESOURCE ASSESSMENT form for you to adapt to your own needs:

... THE COMMITTEE'S RESOURCES

RESOURCE ASSESSMENT FORM

Organization name _____
Address   _____
Phone   _____   Fax _____

President   _____
Address   _____
Phone   _____   Fax _____

Number of members _____
Use of list   _____ YES   _____ times   _____ when
On disk   _____ YES
Donor history   _____ YES

Contributions:
Financial   _____ YES   _____ AMOUNT
    When   _____
Monthly pledge _____ YES   _____ AMOUNT
In-kind   _____
                _____
                _____

National   _____ YES
    Process   _____
                _____

Volunteers
    Number   _____   Services _____

Newsletter
    Contact _____
    Phone   _____   Fax _____

    Deadline _____

Comments _____
_____
_____
_____
_____

POWER IN THE PEOPLE

Using this sample, design a RESOURCE ASSESSMENT form for your group's input:

3

FUND-RAISING

You're asking people to support an important cause. Whether you get a contribution or not has nothing to do with you personally.

A Fund-raising Adage

Committee members should have dollar signs stamped on the palms of their hands. Without enough money, grassroots groups don't accomplish their goals.
   Short-term, achievable goals and creative thinking lead to successful fund-raising.
   Within weeks of the disclosures about Bob Packwood's alleged sexual misconduct, Oregonians for Ethical Representation began holding Celebrating Courage fund-raising events. The events—held in homes in Oregon, and at the Stuart Mott house in Washington, DC, attended by members of Congress—had at least one of the women accusers present to tell her story. The events were win-win-win situations: The women gained confidence and courage from the support of the people present. People got a chance to honor the women. And we were able to raise much

POWER IN THE PEOPLE

needed funds to carry on the campaign against the perceived power and prestige of Bob Packwood who had been in the United States Senate for quarter of a century. In that position, he sent letters to lobbyists and others who needed his help in the Senate, requesting contributions to his legal defense fund. Packwood spent more than $1,000,000 in his defense; most of the contributions to his fund came from outside-Oregon lobbyists. Our grass-roots efforts raised about $60,000, including $10,000 from the DC fund raiser. It was truly a David and Goliath fight!

I learned how to organize this kind of event during the work for passage of the national Equal Rights Amendment in 1977. At that time, the League of Women Voters of the United States gave each state League a fund-raising goal. Our goal in California was $65,000! An unimaginable amount for housewives of the "cookie jar" mentality.

Before our meeting to discuss how to raise so much money, my dear friend, Mary Sandberg, showed us a dramatic documentary about Alice Paul, one of the most remarkable women of this century. Without her single-mindedness and brilliant strategies for gaining American women the right to vote, we might still be waiting.

Among the achievements in her life-long struggle for women's rights, Alice Paul wrote the Equal Rights Amendment in 1923 and started efforts for including gender equality provisions in both the League of Nations and the United Nation Charters. At age eighty, Alice Paul organized the coalition which successfully added equal gender rights to the 1964 Civil Rights Act!

By the end of the movie about Alice Paul, we all felt moved. However, I was moved to act! I stood up with tears running down my checks and said, "If Alice Paul can do all that, we can raise $65,000—and here's how we're going to do it."

The idea captured the imagination and enthusiasm of League members. On January 11, 1978, there were birthday parties for Alice Paul in League members' homes all over California.

FUND-RAISING

Marilyn Juberg, then a college student, donated her beautiful drawing of Alice for the cover of the invitation and designed the inside, too, as her gift to Alice Paul. Leaguers ordered as many invitations as they needed, filled in the blanks on the invitations, held their birthday parties, and sent the California League the proceeds.

We raised $100,000 in one memorable night!

The Lessons we learned by "Just Doing It"

The "Happy Birthday, Alice Paul" concept was successful because it used the most important elements of fund-raising for successful grassroots events.

1. *The project didn't take much time.* Party givers needed only a couple of hours to send invitations and bake a cake.
2. *The idea was creative.* How many "Happy Birthday, Alice Paul" parties have you been invited to?
3. *The $65,000 goal was broken into small, achievable goals.* Here's the formula we put in the LWVC newsletter to show members how we could reach our goal:

HOW CAN WE MAKE A DREAM COME TRUE?

If 10% of the members of LWVC	13,500
	x .10
	1,350 members
hold a party for	20 guests
	27,000 guests
at $5 each	x $5
we raise	$135,000!!!

THAT'S HOW WE MAKE A DREAM COME TRUE!
HAPPY BIRTHDAY, ALICE PAUL!

POWER IN THE PEOPLE

4. *The project was well organized.* Leagues were given all the materials they'd need: a statement giving the reasons for the event; a sample newsletter and news release; an eight-and-one-half-inch by eleven-inch camera-ready copy of the invitation cover drawing of Alice Paul for flyers and other publicity purposes; and, an envelope to send party proceeds to LWVC.
5. *The project was easy.* It didn't require much work from Leaguers who were already busy as wives, mothers, active community leaders, volunteers, returning-to-college students—and, in a very few instances, working full time outside their homes for pay.
6. *The overhead costs were minimal.* No rent. No expensive food or beverages. No costly decorations. No entertainment fees. No facility deposits. It was nearly all profit!
7. *Party givers were committed to the cause.* For each of us, passage of the ERA was the highest priority for action.
8. *The request for attendance was personal.* League members invited their own friends and neighbors.
9. *We increased proceeds by selling ERA items.* T-shirts, bumper stickers, necklaces and bracelets were all available for purchase.

We didn't know much about fund-raising. And we didn't know how to raise $65,000. Instead, we practiced the NIKE motto: Just do it!

But I've started in the middle. On the other hand, isn't that the way we learn life's most important lessons? Still I need to tell you what the beginning is. Let's spend a few minutes talking about the concept of fund-raising.

FUND-RAISING

SUCCESSFUL FUND-RAISING

Fund-raising and budget preparation go hand in hand. It's a chicken-or-an-egg thing. You can't do what you want unless you have enough money; you don't know how much money you'll need until you've developed an Action Plan.

To guide fund-raising, the Action Committee may want to create a Finance Committee to make a Fund-raising Plan. The Plan may include a mix of fund-raising opportunities: mail, events and activities, pledges, personal telephone and mail contact, and one-on-one meetings. Any of these can be directed toward individuals, organizations and political action committees (PACs). Some of the members should have fund-raising experience and others will bring fresh ideas to the group.

Once someone has contributed, they're committed. Be sure you have a plan to ask them every two months— Make it as easy as possible for them to give a second and third time.

Mail

WARNING: "The average rate of return on mass mailing (for candidate campaigns) is 3.5%," according to Jerry Russell, Editor and Publisher, Grass Roots Campaigning (April 1994). Average response to mass mailing on grassroots issues is even less. You may not even cover the costs of your first mailing. But you're informing people about the issue, alerting them that there's an organized group at work, and starting your donor base for asking again. Experienced fund-raisers know the more often you mail to the same potential donors—assuming you have a timely issue, good lists and an effective mail package—the higher your rate of return.

Over years of designing direct mail packages, I've developed a model for successful mass mailings.

POWER IN THE PEOPLE

**Your mail package must standout
from the fistful of other mail in the mailbox.**

1. *The outside envelope is THE most important part of the package.* Fifty percent of all direct mail letters are thrown out *even* with marvelous materials inside!

   - A postage stamp, even the bulk mail kind, gives the envelope a personal look.
   - A telegram format is one way of saying URGENT!
   - The Nature Conservancy used this teaser: *There's one simple thing you can do to save the rain forest . . . Adopt An Acre!*
   - A hand-written teaser—*Important information about your electric bill*—is intriguing.
   - The envelope can give your message—BEWARE: THERE'S A JOB KILLER ON THE NOVEMBER BALLOT! People see the message even if they don't open the envelope.

   Get the person's name and address correct. "If they can't spell my name right, what else won't they get right!"

2. *For your return address, use a street address rather than a post office box.* It gives the sense of permanence. If you use only initials or no name at all, the reader may think it's a personal letter. Be sure your campaign laws don't prohibit this!

3. *The envelope and stationery should be eye-catching.* First impressions are always important. Recruit an art student or professional graphic designer to design these materials as an in-kind contribution to your grassroots cause.

4. *A good graphic on the envelope and stationery adds visual impact.* And it reinforces your message.

5. *Use the letterhead to give credibility and show broad-based and geographic diversity for your cause.* To do this

FUND-RAISING

you can use the left or right margin of your stationary to run a list of your most notable supporters. Remember: In these busy times with lots of very complex issues, many people take positions, not on the facts, but on the credibility of supporters and opponents.

6. *Address the reader by name.* This is easy in the age of computers.
7. *The first sentence must be a grabber.* It may be the only part of the letter a "skimmer" reads.
8. *Speak to the reader.* The letter must address the self interest of the reader.
9. *Give facts.* Give enough facts so readers feel confident they're making an informed decision. But not too many. That's overwhelming, confusing and boring.
10. *Get to the point.* I like one-page letters. They make the message concise, focused and clear—so the reader is more apt to get it. But a lot of others prefer longer—even four-page letters. The decision may depend on your audience: Do they get their information mostly from reading or from television? Do they like lots of facts? Is this your first letter to them?
11. *Make the letter easy to read.* Use short sentences. Short paragraphs. Bullets. Underline key points. Lots of white space.
12. *Use power-packed, persuasive language.* People give when they feel emotional.
13. *Always ask for specific amounts.* You'll help the reader know what's expected.
14. *Have the letter signed by more than one person.* This is another way to show credibility and diversity.
15. *The P.S. is almost certain to be read.* In fact, one mail expert says it's the most often read part of a letter.
16. *Add one enclosure that gives your cause credibility.* It

POWER IN THE PEOPLE

makes the package look substantial. Copies of newspaper editorials, political cartoons, pictures are good enclosures.

17. *Enclose a self-addressed contribution envelope.* You're using an important fund-raising adage: Make it as easy as possible to give. If your funds are limited, instead of having envelopes printed, copy the text on colored paper. Use plain, three-and-one-half inch by six-and-one-half inch envelopes and a rubber stamp or a label to put your mailing address on the front. That's a good job for children—you're teaching them that "Democracy is not a spectator sport."

Total weight of the package, including the outside envelope cannot exceed one ounce—or you pay extra postage.

And, of course, you should have a pledge card to hand out at meetings.

YES on #1 for PARKS AND JOBS
MAJOR DONOR PLEDGE FORM

I will support the YES on #1 for PARKS AND JOBS Campaign by:

____ Making a personal contribution of $_____ now.

____ Authorizing a contribution from my company of $_____ now.

____ Pledging to raise $_____ by (insert dates 2 weeks away)

I will meet my pledge by:

____ Conducting personal one-on-one meetings.

____ Making personal phone calls.

____ Sending a personal letter and following up with phone calls.

____ Hosting a breakfast, lunch, reception or an event at my home.

____ Selling tickets to YES on #1 for PARKS AND JOBS fundraising events. I will sell tickets at the $100____ $250____ or $500 ____ levels.

____ Providing names of potential donors and/or volunteers.

____ Providing space for phone banks at my company.

____ And, of course, you may use may name publicly on campaign materials.

FUND-RAISING

First Class vs. Third Class or Bulk Mail, as it's sometimes called

There are two schools of thought. One school says, "If you treat your mail like junk mail, so will the people who receive it. Send it first class." Others say it depends on how current your lists are, how important the issue is to people on those lists, how good your mail package is, and how many people you plan to mail to.

For specific information on requirements and costs check with your local post office, but here are some general guidelines.

First Class Mail

Use it when you're mailing to less than 200 people or if fast delivery is critical.

Normally first class takes only one or two days for local delivery. Mail that can't be delivered will be returned to you at no additional cost. By using this returned mail to update your data base, you're building a list for future use.

Third Class or Bulk Mail

Use it when you're mailing to more than 200, timing isn't so important, you have either enough volunteers or can afford to pay a mail house to do the processing.

Normally third class mail takes at least two days for local delivery—and my colleague, Frank Schubert, reminds me it usually takes a *lot* longer! Mail that can't be delivered will be returned to you *only* if your envelope states ADDRESS CORRECTION REQUESTED *and* if you pay first class postage for each returned letter—that's very expensive if the lists you're using are old.

Some Random Thoughts on Mass Mailing

If you plan to mail to several thousand potential donors, consider mailing to 500 people first. This test marketing strategy will help you learn if your package works—or if you have a dud.

35

POWER IN THE PEOPLE

In case you don't get a good response, reevaluate your package, change parts of it based upon your evaluation, consider the quality of the lists you used—and you'll save money. You may even need to consider whether you've hit the right time for this issue and whether the issue has enough supporters to make mass mailing profitable.

Estimating Results

The formula for estimating results is fairly accurate. Within four days after "dropping" a first class mailing or seven to eight days for a third class mailing, contributions will begin to arrive. Five days after the first receipts have arrived your mailing will peak. Multiply your total contributions by two. That's an estimated total you can expect to get from the mailing.

Now take the total dollar amount of contributions and divide that by the total number of contributions you received. That's the average contribution for this mailing—an amount to use to estimate returns from future mailings.

Follow Up

To build good relations with donors, it's important to send thank you notes ASAP; my goal is sending notes within two days of receiving the contribution. With grassroots efforts and for contributions under one hundred dollars, I use a simple postcard. It's inexpensive to produce, postage costs less, precious volunteer time is saved for more important work.

To qualify for the postcard postage rate, the card must not be larger than six inches by four-and one-fourth inches.

Here's a sample card I designed. Please feel free to adapt it to your purposes:

FUND-RAISING

> **Women's Legal Advocacy Fund**
> **PO Box 2190 Portland, OR 97208-2190**
>
> Dear Friend,
>
> During this last phase of the "Packwood matter," your generous contribution is more important than ever.
>
> Your continuing support gives the women confidence that they are surrounded by men and women who have stood with them throughout this challenging and unprecedented experience.
>
> On behalf of the women and their attorneys, most grateful thanks for Celebrating their Courage.

We had this card copied on colored cardstock at a neighborhood copy shop. Each card was signed by a member of the Committee who knew the contributor. In larger efforts, the cards could be signed by a volunteer above a printed line: "Another Volunteer for (whatever your cause—Greenspaces, Good Schools)."

Contributors of more than one hundred dollars may expect a personal letter from the Committee's Chairperson—I learned this lesson the hard way!

Events and Activities

The choices for fund-raising events are as endless as your imagination! Ask these questions:

1. Who do we want to attract?

2. How much would they pay?

3. What would appeal to them?

POWER IN THE PEOPLE

Invitations

Whatever the event, invitations must include a description of the event, a description of the cause, and complete information about the event: who is holding it; where, include name of place, street address and city; day, date, and time; double check your date and day to the calendar; cost; a telephone number for more information; whether the event is tax deductible; whom to make the check payable to; and where to send it—just in case the self-addressed envelope you enclose is lost.

And follow-up phoning is crucial for success!

House parties

Events like "Alice Paul Birthday Parties" are called "house parties." They're at-home events—simple as you like or as fancy as you have the resources to pull off. Usually the event givers provide the place, food and entertainment or program. They may also set the price for their event or there may be a fixed price.

A wonderful model is an annual event in Portland. "Dinner at My House for Our House," is sponsored by Our House of Portland, a residential care facility for people living and dying with AIDS. In 1994, "22 hosts opened their wonderful homes to some very special evenings of dining."

- "Get the French Vanilla 'scoop,'" given by a francophile & local columnist
- "Dinner at 8," reliving the golden era of the 30s . . . dress the part if you like
- "Cocktails and Dinner Overlooking the Moon Garden"
- "Summer Whites," wear white for an old-fashioned croquet party in the afternoon
- "Political Fare," by a State Representative
- "Southern Comfort," showcasing fine cuisines, wine and art
- "Garden Tent Party," dining under the big top in a world of horticulture

FUND-RAISING

- "Anchors Aweigh," cocktails on a scenic cruise, then a sumptuous feast
- "Eastern European Dinner," Hungarian fare at its finest
- "Hawaiian BBQ," for people in Hawaiian shirts or mumus
- "Elegant Evening," dinner by candlelight in one of the city's most beautiful homes
- "Spanish Cuisine," feast on paella and other tantalizing dishes
- "A 'Belle Epoque' Dinner a la Proust," a Parisian dinner from the turn of the century
- "The Great Gatsby," reliving one of the Great-Gatsby-era dinner parties
- "Christmas at Our House," Holiday treats at the start of the Season and a request to bring a gift for one of the folks at Our House
- " Yule-Do," stepping back in history for an old-fashioned European Christmas

Isn't that a great list of party themes? But if one doesn't grab you, then look at these categories of themes and find one that works with your issue: nations, movies, seasons, holidays, famous authors or people, eras, music, mysteries, pioneers, dances, sports events, childhood memories. Be creative!

Concerts

The most memorable fund-raising event of the 1990 Oregon pro-choice campaign was an evening of chamber music performed by Portland Symphony members—who called and asked what they could do to help the cause. The concert was held in a fabulous gallery. The "final chorus" of the evening consisted of sinfully fattening desserts donated by some of the city's best chefs served from tables decorated with stunning, donated centerpieces.

POWER IN THE PEOPLE

Any kind of musical event with any kind of music by local talent or nationally known musicians are fund-raising event options. Be sure the talent is worth hearing and their style is appropriate for the audience you hope will come. Ask the performers if they'll waive their normal fee. Or reduce it. If not, then ask if they'll contribute a portion of their fee to the event. Any of these will help cut your overhead costs and it's good public relations for them.

Make a list of fund-raising events that you think would be appropriate for your cause and the people you want to attend.

_____
_____
_____

Whom to Invite

Invite everyone who could be interested in your cause and might spend the money to attend a wonderful party.

1. *For house parties invite at least twice as many people as you can handle.* Having too many people is a wonderful problem!

2. *For larger, more public events where invitations are sent to special friends, organization membership lists and your contributor base, invite hundreds more than you can handle.* The rule of thumb: three percent of people invited will attend.

Use the following list to start brain-storming:

- Men and women
- Friends
- Teachers
- People you work with
- Parents of your children's friends
- People from your church
- Professionals
- Youth leaders
- Neighbors
- Friends of friends
- Members of organizations
- People you send Holiday cards to
- People in government
- Labor union members
- Political party activists
- Others

FUND-RAISING

And invite people from the media for free if you want the community to know what a success you've had.

Make a list of people and categories of people you think would want to be invited to your event.

_____
_____
_____

Timeline

With special thanks to Suone Cotner, the best fund-raiser I've ever worked with, on the following page is a timeline for events planning. When Suone led the fund-raising part of the 1990 pro-choice campaign in Oregon, she designed and implemented a plan that raised more than $1,000,000.

Random Thoughts About the Timeline

1. *Media.*
   If your event is open to the public, be sure to give the details to the calendar reporters and to reporters covering your issue (environmental, business, political, government, etc.) for your local papers and radio stations in advance. You may also want to remind them on the day of the event. They will expect to be your guests.

2. *Sponsors.*
   These "angels" have "names" that will help attract guests. Or they may cover the up-front costs of the event. Or they may totally fund the event.

3. *Captains.*
   These terrific people take responsibility for selling a certain number of tickets. Ten tickets is a realistic number to start with.

POWER IN THE PEOPLE

EVENT_____ CHAIR(S)_____
DATE_____ TICKET PRICE_____
LOCATION_____ GOAL_____

4 - 6 weeks before the event   Date:_____
    1. Set the date
    2. Select the location/reserve facility
    3. Select and schedule speaker/talent
    4. Establish ticket price and $ goal
    5. Determine sources of appropriate guest lists
    6. Recruit sponsors and captains
    7. Establish committees and recruit chairs: ticket sellers, food, beverages, decorations, set-up, sign-in, serving, clean-up, etc.
    8. Design the invitation. Consider including purpose of event

4 - 5 weeks before the event   Date:_____
    1. Produce the invitation
    2. Obtain mailing lists
    3. Prepare mailing
    4. Recruit volunteers for phone follow up
    5. Recruit ticket sellers

3 - 4 weeks before the event   Date:_____
    1. Arrange for food and beverages
    2. Hold ticket sellers' meeting
    3. Mail the invitations

3 weeks before the event   Date:_____
    1. Schedule follow-up phoning
    2. Check progress of captains and ticket sellers

2 weeks before the event   Date:_____
    1. Check progress of captains and ticket sellers
    2. Confirm all arrangements: location, food, beverage, decorations, speaker/talent, etc.
    3. Obtain banquet permit, if necessary
    4. Begin follow-up phoning

1 week before the event   Date:_____
    1. Continue follow-up phoning
    2. Get report from captains and ticket sellers
    3. Recruit volunteers for sign-in table, serving, clean-up, etc.

Day before the event   Date:_____
    1. Prepare list of reservations; pre-paid, pay at the door
    2. Prepare sign-in sheets, name tags, etc.
    3. Make last minute check of all arrangements
    4. Confirm all scheduled volunteers

THE DAY   Volunteers arrive before the event and stay until its over. Raise money! Have fun! Be sure all cash contributions are clearly noted for the treasurer.

ASAP   Send thank you notes to everyone who helped in even the smallest way!

FUND-RAISING

OTHER FUND-RAISING OPPORTUNITIES

We could fill volumes with fund-raising possibilities. Here are a few for you to consider.

1. *Raffles.* Your community or state may have rules governing raffles. Find out what they are from your city attorney before you start planning this common moneymaker.
2. *Auctions.* To be successful, auctions take an enormous amount of planning, work and follow up—but many organizations find them worth the effort.
3. *Non-parties.* Members of my church just sent fifteen dollars for a Non-Buffet and twenty dollars more for an Optional String Quartet Non-Concert. We didn't get dressed up. We didn't go anywhere. We just sent money.
4. *Walks and Runs.* Perhaps a supporter with experience in organizing runs can bring in the gold for your cause.
5. *Entertainment Books.* Here's a win-win-win situation. Consumers benefit with discount coupons for restaurants, travel accommodations, and activities. Community organizations profit from sales of these books. Participating merchants increase their business.
6. *Business Support.* During a "Green Weekend" in Portland, Oregon, merchants and restaurants gave 10 percent of their net proceeds to the Metropolitan Greenspaces ballot measure campaign.
7. *Scrip.* My church and lots of other non-profit organizations are selling scrip. Parishioners buy the scrip at church and then use it like money at participating merchants, including major grocery and department stores. The organizations get a percentage of the face value of the scrip.
8. *Selling Tamales and Other Good Things.* When members of churches in Huntington Beach, California, formed a

POWER IN THE PEOPLE

Head Start, the Spanish-speaking mothers, led by dynamic and spirited Alice Medina, made traditional tamales to raise funds. What special gifts do your supporters have that would bring cultural diversity to the fund-raising efforts in your community?

Of course, there are lots of other things you can sell—T-shirts, buttons, bumper stickers, and jewelry to name but a few. My experience is that these don't make much money, but they make supporters feel good and they help build awareness of the issue.

PLEDGES

One of the best ways of ensuring regular cash flow is to get commitments for monthly pledges. Maybe this is one of the requirements for serving on your Action Committee. If there are ten people on the Committee who pledge five dollars a month, you have fifty dollars a month. That's more than enough to get a local, grassroots citizens action committee started, handle routine mailing, copying and phone costs and perhaps have some to save for other needs later.

PHONE AND PERSONAL LETTER CONTACTS

Personal phone and letter "asking" is considered second best to one-on-one meetings. But "that ain't necessarily so."

Former Justice of the Oregon Supreme Court and my soul sister in the "Packwood matter," Betty Roberts, picks up the phone and gets amazing results. She's successful because she has credibility and is highly respected. Betty knows her "audience," and she's Texas-gracious in her direct fund-raising approach.

FUND-RAISING

Even more important: She isn't afraid of rejection! She asks for what she wants—and most often gets it.

ONE-ON-ONE SOLICITATIONS

Many people are frightened by one-on-one meetings with potential major donors. It's important to get over fears because one-on-ones offer the greatest potential for large dollar results. Once you get the hang of them, you may find them challenging fun!

"Fun?" you ask. Yes, if you see challenges as games with players, maneuvers, strategies. Or as graceful dances with people moving together in harmony toward a shared goal.

Like other new adventures, you'll gain confidence by breaking the job into small parts. To be successful requires:

1. *Research.* What is this person's commitment in this cause? Has she or he given before? How much? When? What other causes does she or he support? Who is the best person to do the asking? How much does he or she give to those causes?

   People new to fund-raising often ask how to determine a "reasonable" amount. One way is by knowing the people you're asking and the community pattern of giving. In some cases, like the 1994 NO on Amendment 6 Arkansas campaign, the finance committee established a formula: each employer was asked to contribute $7.50 for each employee.

   Perhaps the following form will help you begin to feel organized and in control.

POWER IN THE PEOPLE

MAJOR DONOR CONTACT FORM

Solicitor:_____
Date Due:_____
Pledge Amt.:_____
Thank you sent_____

Name:_____ O ( )_____
Title:_____ H ( )_____
Company/Organization:_____
Goal:_____
Office Address:_____
City, State, Zip:_____
Home Address:_____
City, State, Zip:_____
Referred by:_____ Status Call:_____
Donor History:_____
Notes:_____
_____
_____

CONTACT #1
Date:_____ Phone:_____ Meeting:_____
Comments:_____
_____
_____

CONTACT #2
Date:_____ Phone:_____ Meeting:_____
Comments:_____
_____
_____

CONTACT #3
Date:_____ Phone:_____ Meeting:_____
Comments:_____
_____
_____

FUND-RAISING

2. *Preparation.* Potential major donors want their contributions to be well spent. You can help assure them by being prepared for your meeting. Give them an information packet. Use simple, twin pocket portfolios available at office supply discount stores for less than thirty cents apiece.
   - In the left pocket put things that will give your group credibility—materials about your issue: fact sheets, editorials, endorsements.
   - In the right pocket put information related to the grassroots organization: a summary of your Campaign Plan, a budget, names of the Action Committee members.
   - Be sure there's a contribution envelope.
3. *An appointment.* Your side of the telephone conversation might sound something like this: "Mrs. Angel, this is Cathy Cause. My friend and yours, (name of person who suggested you call) thought you would be interested in an important issue I'm working on in our community. I wonder if I could have less than thirty minutes of your time next week. I'd like to give you information about (name your cause)." "Would Tuesday or Wednesday be better for you?" "Would you like to meet in the morning or after lunch?" (An option: "I work full time, so it would be best for me if we could have breakfast together or meet for coffee late in the afternoon. Would either of those work for you?") "Shall we meet in your office? Or would you rather meet somewhere for tea?" "That's fine. I have your office address as 123 Any Street. Is that correct?" "Wonderful. I look forward to seeing you in your office at ten o'clock next Wednesday, the twenty-third of September. Thank you. Good bye."

People know you're coming to ask for something. If they aren't open to giving, they won't make an appointment.

POWER IN THE PEOPLE

4. *A Meeting.* Introduce yourself. Thank the person for meeting with you. Spend just a few minutes in "getting-to-know-you" conversation. Then open the packet and go through the pages one at a time. Because your packet is in logical order, you'll move through the meeting with ease. The meeting will:

- *Establish your credibility* as a knowledgeable, poised community leader.
- *Explain the issue* and why it's important.
- *Offer proof of a soundly managed effort.*
- *Give the "angel" a chance to ask questions.*
- *Tell the person specifically what you want.*

"Mrs. Angel, can we count on you for a contribution of (specific amount)?" . . . "That's wonderful!" . . . "Will you write a check now or will you send it later?". . . "It will help us with cash-flow planning if we know whether to expect your contribution this month or next." . . . "Thank you so much for your time and your generosity." . . . "Good bye."

During the meeting, keep the discussion on the subject—remember, you've made a commitment to take less than thirty minutes.

5. *A thank you note.* Send a thank you note ASAP. Someone who has given you their valuable time, even if they didn't make a commitment, deserves a personal thank you note. This sensitive gesture may help set the stage to get a contribution later.

6. *Staying in touch.* Major donors are an important part of your team! Send them a regular STATUS REPORT. Invite them to special events. Ask them to help you raise money. Give them advance notice of good news and bad news. Offer them opportunities to contribute again.

FUND-RAISING

Phone Banks

For greatest returns, all fund-raising efforts—mass mailings, events, activities, personal contact—require personal phone calls to follow up within ten days. Returns from mailings, for example, can increase as much as 25 percent with follow up phoning. Nancy Farrar, a champion phone bank organizer, knows that results are greatest when:

1. *Phoners are in one location.* They feel they're part of a team. The lists don't get lost and you have assurance the calls are made. Offices are often donated as in-kind contributions for phone banking.
2. *You're well prepared, well organized and relaxed.*
3. *You provide light refreshments and drinks.* That helps phoners feel comfortable for a short, simple briefing. They need to hear why this cause is important and how vital their work is.
4. *During the briefing each phoner is given a packet* that includes:
    - a list of people who were sent the mailing but haven't yet contributed;
    - a card with codes to be put next to the name of each person after they have been phoned:

    (Y = will send; N = won't send; NC = no contact);
    - answers to commonly asked questions;
    - a script for phoners practice before they start calling. They read the script aloud and do some role playing so they learn to "talk the talk."
5. *Calls are made on Sundays and weekdays between 6:30 PM and 9:00 PM and on Saturdays between 10:00 AM and noon.* This may vary from season to season and in different regions of the country. One thing that doesn't vary: If

POWER IN THE PEOPLE

you're trying to reach men, DO *NOT* CALL ON MONDAY EVENINGS DURING FOOTBALL SEASON or on SUPER BOWL SUNDAY!

6. *Phone scripts are short.* Calls should take less than five minutes—enough time to give the purpose of the call without being terse or annoying. The motto: BE POLITE, ASSERTIVE, APPRECIATIVE.

Here's a sample phone script for you to adapt to your own cause:

PHONE SCRIPT

Hello. Is this _____? (Their name), this is (your name). I'm calling on behalf of the Women's Legal Advocacy Fund.

Did you get the letter we sent you recently about our efforts to support the women who have told about Bob Packwood's acts of sexual misconduct against them?

IF "YES" Then you know we appreciate your past support—but we need your help again.

Have you had a chance to let your two U.S. Senators know you want public hearings?

IF "YES" That's terrific!
IF "NO" Do you need their addresses?

IF "NO" In its preliminary investigation, the Senate Ethics Committee has concluded "there is substantial evidence" that Sen. Packwood engaged in sexual misconduct, altered evidence, and used his office to inappropriately link personal financial gain to his official position. But the Committee has not yet called for public hearings.

FUND-RAISING

That's why we need your help again.

Will you let your two U.S. Senators know you want public hearings?

IF "YES"   That's terrific! Do you need their addresses?

IF "NO"   Then can you help in another way?

TO ALL   Can we count on you to make another generous contribution to help the women? We must be able to do whatever is necessary to get public hearings—mailings, newspaper ads—and to be sure if there are public hearings, that the women are accompanied by their volunteer attorneys.

IF "YES   Confirm name and address.

Thanks so much! You're helping make a place that's free of sexual misconduct for our daughters and granddaughters.

Processing Contributions

The correct handling of funds is essential to building and maintaining the credibility of your group and its work. Recruit a professional bookkeeper or accountant to:

1. *Receive all contributions*—checks and cash;
2. *Arrange the checks in alphabetical order*;
3. *Make at least one copy of the face of each check* for the Committee; and,
4. *Make all bank deposits.*

The Committee and everyone working on its behalf must obey the laws for reporting contributions and expenditures for

POWER IN THE PEOPLE

political issues and it must follow standard business practices. Recruit a reliable volunteer to do the tasks above. Be sure that your money is handled and accounted for and bank reconciliations are done by two different people.

Since we seldom know at the beginning of an effort how long it's going to last, it's a good idea to build a contribution history for every contributor. The history gives you background that takes some of the guess work out of asking for future contributions.

Notice from the Internal Revenue Service

If a donation is for a political issue, it is usually not tax deductible. Check before you tell people their contributions will be or won't be deductible.

If, however, contributions to your effort are deductible, and if a person gets something of value in return for a contribution, the *only* part of the contribution that is deductible is the amount that is more than the fair market value of the benefit or merchandise. An Internal Revenue Service publication says, "You should decide in advance the fair value of any benefit or merchandise to be given to contributors and tell them when you publicize the fund-raising event or solicit their contributions how much is deductible and how much is for the benefit or merchandise."

Here's what the Liberty Hill Foundation and Hollywood Policy Center put on the bottom of their thank you note for the tickets I bought for the World Premiere of *How To Make An American Quilt*. The proceeds of the spectacular event are being used for two programs working to improve the lives of women, children and families.

> We estimate that the fair market value of each ticket to attend the premiere event was $32. The amount of your contribution that is deductible for federal income tax purposes is limited

FUND-RAISING

to the excess of the money you paid over the value of the tickets you received or were available to you. Your deductible contribution is $_____. If you donated any tickets back to Liberty Hill prior to the event, you may increase your contribution by $32 per ticket donated. Liberty Hill's Tax ID #_____.

For more details get Internal Revenue Service Publication 1391, *Deductibility of Payments Made to Charities Conducting Fund-Raising Events.*

And remember, if the donation is for a political issue, it is usually *not* deductible. Currently, however, tax laws allow businesses to deduct such expenditures as legitimate business expenses. Check before you tell people their contributions will be tax deductible.

4

PUBLIC DISCLOSURE, FINANCE REPORTS, AND TAX STATUS

Always do right. This will gratify some and astonish the rest.

Mark Twain

Your Action Committee must obey all rules and regulations. You must find out if you are required to register the Committee and report all contributions and expenditures. It's vital that you and the other leaders of the Action Committee completely understand all regulations that govern your activities. It's also vital to find out if your organization must file with the Internal Revenue Service!

Ask an attorney or accountant experienced in campaign laws to be your volunteer guide through the maze of campaign regulations. With professional guidance, you'll avoid making innocent mistakes that may damage your cause's credibility, may be perceived as dishonest, and can cost you money for fines.

POWER IN THE PEOPLE

PUBLIC DISCLOSURE AND DISCLAIMERS

In many areas, committees that lobby or work on political issues or elections—either candidate or ballot measure—must file papers of organization *before they receive or spend any money*. These papers tell who the officers are and what the organization's purpose is.

Until a 1995 United States Supreme Court ruling, committees were required to put information about their organization—called a "disclaimer"—on political materials. The Court said that requirement infringed on the First Amendment right of freedom of speech. States are now figuring out how to respond to this ruling. Required or not by law, the name and address of the Action Committee on materials shows you have nothing to hide and you're proud of your cause!

CONTRIBUTION AND EXPENDITURE REPORTING

Action Committees may also be required to report who contributed; how much they contributed; whether the contribution was cash, in-kind, or a loan; and how funds were spent. There may be limits on contributions and restrictions on in-kind contributions.

Call your City Clerks' Office *and* your Secretary of State's Office to find out:

Is your Action Committee required to file organization papers?
If yes:
What information is needed? _____
When is it filed? _____
Where is it filed? _____
What are the campaign finance laws
that govern your cause? _____

PUBLIC DISCLOSURE . . .

Is there a community forum on campaign finance laws? _____
May you attend? When? Where? _____
Is there a cost? _____

What about contribution and expenditure reporting?
What information must you file? _____
Where do you get forms? _____
Are the forms on computer disk? _____
If yes, how do you get a copy? _____
If not, do they approve the format your
committee plans to use? _____
What are the reporting dates? _____
      Put those dates on your Master Calendar!

TAX STATUS

While most Action Committees don't qualify for tax exempt status, it's worth asking about.
• 501(c)(3) status is for "charitable, religious, educational, scientific, literary, testing for public safety, fostering national or international amateur sports competition . . . prevention of cruelty to children or animals."
• 501(c)(4) status is for "civic leagues and social welfare organizations."

Political Action Committees (PACs) are not "charitable" and, therefore, are not deductible as charitable contributions on federal taxes and may or may not be on your state taxes. Businesses, however, may be able to deduct such expenditures as legitimate business expenses.
To get expert advice on the laws and regulations that apply to your Action Committee may cost you a little money if you can't find someone to do it free—but it's worth the peace of mind

POWER IN THE PEOPLE

and allows you to focus your attention and energy on your important issue. This is no place to cut corners, put compliance off, or be sloppy!

5

GETTING ALL THE FACTS

The response of Enrico Caruso, one of the great tenors of all time, to the question: What do you think of your contemporary, Babe Ruth?

"I don't know. I haven't heard her sing."

Clearly Caruso didn't have all the facts! But you're not Caruso (he died in 1921). You must have the facts—favorable and unfavorable, pro and con—regarding your issue if you want to be politically effective. You want to know:

1. *Its history.* Has this issue been a problem? Why? Why hasn't it been solved? Who were the players? What were the messages? Which of them worked and which didn't? (Keep a record of the messages. You may want to test them through a survey.)

2. *All sides.* Can you redefine your goal so it appeals to more people? Or to avoid polarizing your community? Or to neutralize the opposition?

3. *How the government works.* Who drafts the laws? Who has input? Are there public hearings? Is there a timeline?

POWER IN THE PEOPLE

Will the budget be affected? If yes, is there money? Can you show how there could be long-term savings for a short-term expenditure?

4. *How elected officials stand on the issue.* Have they voted on this issue before? If yes, how did they vote? Was it a campaign issue? How do their largest contributors feel about the issue?

5. *If the issue has been covered by local media.* What reporters covered it? Did they get the facts straight?

6. *If there have been editorial positions.* Who took them? What were the positions?

Through the process of getting answers to all the questions you can think of, you'll learn where to go for help and what to avoid. You'll identify allies, potential supporters and opponents, and strong opponents, especially among influential opinion leaders, people in government, elected officials, their staff members, and the media. You'll be in a good position to be effective and to avoid being blindsided. And, because you're building a position of strength based on facts, you'll be building your confidence, too!

The League of Women Voters taught me how to get this kind of information. If you're lucky enough to have a League in your community, think about starting there. Call and ask who in the League is most knowledgeable about your issue and ask to meet with her. In addition to the League, other good sources of facts are your local library, the chamber of commerce, political parties and people familiar with the issue.

One of the traits of successful people is that they ask for help. Pick up the phone and call five people who will have different points of view. Tell them you're doing a political analysis of your community on the issue of (name your issue) and you'd like their input. Because you'll be well prepared and organized, you'll need less than thirty minutes of their time.

GETTING ALL THE FACTS

When I go into a state to manage a ballot measure campaign, here are the questions I ask:

1. Who is on our side?
2. Who is the opposition?
3. What is the history of the issue?
4. Where can I get a file of clippings on the issue? Then I get the file and read every clipping.
5. What polling has been done? And I study the results.
6. What public disclosure and campaign finance regulations apply? Have all the proper reports been filed? What are the plans to ensure compliance?

Make a list of the questions you need to get answered. And remember to keep asking questions. Every question should make you think of more questions. By the time you're through, you'll have a thorough understanding of the issue.

I've kept this part of our conversation brief because—while getting facts is important—we shouldn't use the process as a delaying tactic. Sometimes people who lack confidence do that.

**You want an honest political assessment.
For this part of your work, put aside your own opinion.
You'll be able to hear better!**

6

POLLING

Failure is impossible!

Alice Paul

Is polling really necessary? On small local issues, such as a stop sign on the corner, no. But the more complex the issue and the more citizens deciding on the issue, the more emphatic the YES!

Look at the results of a poll taken shortly after the O.J. Simpson verdict. The following table, "Misperceptions about U.S. Population," was recently published by the *Washington Post*.

Q: What percentage of the U.S. Population is . . .

(responses from:	Whites	Blacks	Asians	Hispanics)	1992 census data
. . . WHITE?	49.9%	45.5%	54.8%	46.7%	74%
. . . BLACK?	23.8%	25.9%	20.5%	22.7%	11.8%
. . . HISPANIC?	14.7%	16.3%	14.6%	20.7%	9.5%
. . . ASIAN?	10.8%	12.2%	8.3%	10.8%	3.1%

sources: Washington Post/Kaiser Family Foundation/Harvard University survey, U.S. Census Bureau

POWER IN THE PEOPLE

If so many of us are so far off on facts about the ethnic makeup of our nation, then we surely will be even farther off on less tangible things like the general public's attitudes on issues. That's why polling is so important to laying out an effective campaign plan.

Polling—public opinion research, research, surveys, they're just different words for the same thing—helps you in four major ways:

1. It gives you a snapshot of what public attitudes about your issue are at the moment the research is conducted.

2. It provides the basis for planning your strategy.

3. If thorough, it tells you whether people agree with you about the problem; it also tells you what solutions to the problem people will agree to. One of the frustrations elected officials in Washington have had with both health care reform and balancing the federal budget is that, while Americans overwhelmingly agree there's a problem, there isn't a consensus on the solutions.

4. It helps you avoid falling into BIG traps! Committee members will want to substitute their own attitudes or anecdotes—personal experiences—for the general public's attitudes. They'll want the campaign to switch strategies and messages to respond to their own beliefs. Polling results show them what the public attitudes are—and they help you keep everyone using the correct messages.

Think about it this way. Do you remember what your childhood world was like or how you felt before you learned to read? At least half—perhaps as many as 90 percent—of the people you need to talk to aren't "reading" your issue yet—or, if they are, their minds can be changed for the right reasons.

You need to know what one, two, or three reasons—messages—will make these people "read" your issue and move to

POLLING

your side, who the people are who will move to your side and where they get their information about issues. That's where polling comes in.

Polling scientifically measures opinions based on a sample of voters. That sample proportionately represents your target audience: people who will be affected by an issue like property taxes to buy greenspaces, or who will vote on a ballot measure. The sample, often based on census data and voter information lists, includes men and women from different ethnic, age, and income groups who live in different areas and belong to different political parties. These characteristics are called "demographics." The sample must match the demographic patterns in the population if the survey results are to be accurate. Responses to survey questions and the demographic information are usually gathered in telephone interviews which are often as long as twenty minutes.

To get accurate responses, a survey is written so people being polled don't know which side of an issue is taking the survey. Interviewers:

1. Don't know who is paying for the poll.
2. Are unbiased.
3. Never try to persuade people to change their minds.
4. Are friendly but professional.
5. Ask questions and get people's reactions to new information about an issue. The best interviewers are like human tape recorders, accurately reporting respondents' answers without embellishing them with their own nuances.

Polling tells you who your audience is; what messages—both pro and con—are most persuasive; what spokespersons are most credible with the audience; and from which mediums—television, radio, print—they get information about issues.

POWER IN THE PEOPLE

Polls are written to tell you:
1. *What the public already knows about the issue.* "Have you heard about (name the issue)?" "What have you heard?" (two or three questions)
2. *What the public thinks about the issue.* "Are you for or against this issue?" You need to know what demographic groups are for, against, and are still undecided on your issue. (one question)
3. *What messages are most persuasive and powerful.* "I'm going to read you some reasons why people favor or oppose this issue. Please tell me whether you have a positive or negative reaction to each one." (The number of questions depends on the complexity of the issue.)

There are usually lots of good reasons for people to take either side of an issue. You must find the one, two, or three that work best with the people who aren't your supporters *yet*.

Be sure to test the other side's messages. It's important to know what your opponents may use to sell their position. If you do, you can anticipate and be prepared to counter what they may say.

4. *After hearing all the messages, now how do they feel about the issue.* When the results are analyzed, you'll find out what demographic groups will move from leaning for, leaning against, and undecided to your position. And you'll know which messages will move them.
(one question)

On this question, your point of view needs to be well above 60 percent to have a chance of winning against strong opposition!

5. *Who these people listen to.* "Now, I'm going to give you the names of some people and organizations who may

POLLING

speak for or against (name the issue). Please tell me which ones you'd believe when they talk about this issue."
(ten to sixteen names)

Spokespersons are most believable when they have experience on the subject and when their profession relates to the issue. For example, on an issue favoring storage of low-level nuclear waste in Nebraska the leading spokespersons included a past president of the Sierra Club and the Dean of the School of Medicine at Creighton University. They were key in taking an "unbeatable measure" to defeat with 64 percent of the vote.

In looking at "believability," check the level of both positive and negative attitudes. Someone may have very high positive, but if he or she has 25 percent negative, think twice before having him or her as general public spokesperson. They may be terrific, though, with certain audiences.

6. *What mediums to use.* "Where do you get most of your news? Television? Radio? Newspaper? Friends? (four questions)

Focus Groups and Advertising Tests

Other types of public opinion research include focus groups and advertising tests. Unlike telephone surveys where a random sample of people are phoned, focus groups consist of discussions with a small group of individuals. Typically people gather in a central facility for two-hour discussions with groups of ten people

Focus groups and advertisement testing follow the same general format, but have different purposes. They are usually groups of frequent voters who have been recruited by phone and invited to join in a group discussion on an issue—not disclosed until early in the discussion. Participants are paid thirty-five dollars to fifty dollars for attending.

POWER IN THE PEOPLE

Focus groups are facilitated by a low-key, skilled discussion leader who identifies basic community values and attitudes, and probes for in-depth opinions and potential messages on the issue. Christopher Herbert, President of The Insight Group, is extraordinarily skilled in designing formats for focus groups and as a discussion leader. Participants never know if he has an opinion on the subject, what that opinion is, or who is paying for the group. This information might bias the discussion.

Focus groups are used to get a basic understanding of community values and attitudes on the issue. It was in a focus group conducted by the National Abortion Rights Action League (NARAL), that a participant pointed out that the issue isn't abortion, it's about who makes the choice. That's how framing the issue became pro-choice versus pro-life.

Ad testing, often done in groups of fifty voters, gets audience response to television ad concepts or finished spots. People watch the concepts or spots and grade them on level of factual content, believability, and persuasiveness.

In 1993, Goddard Claussen/First Tuesday, the firm I work with, tested a series of spots. The tests showed that, while the message worked, the spots weren't powerful enough to move large groups of voters. The spots were changed to have the spokespersons admit they wanted health care reform; they just didn't like the proposed solution. These revised spots—the famous "Harry and Louise" spots—were so powerful they redefined the debate about the Clinton health care plan and changed the dialogue on health care in the nation.

In one campaign I managed in Oregon, we had produced spots and were shocked when the spot we professional managers liked most was a dud with the ad-test group. During the discussion after respondents had seen the spots, we learned that the audience was turned off by the doctor's Australian accent! If we hadn't done the test, we'd have been on the air with a spot about which voters had very negative feelings.

POLLING

Professional or Volunteer Pollster

Doing polling right means getting hundreds of details right. None of these details is particularly hard to grasp, or hard to get right. Getting all of them right is difficult, particularly if you have to rely on volunteers or people who don't have experience in polling.

A professional pollster gives you the benefits of expertise in designing surveys, use of trained interviewers, the ability to manage responses to hundreds of surveys, and experience in analyzing and accurately interpreting survey results.

Equally important, a professional pollster has the ability to get interviews with an accurate demographic balance. A sample of 400 voters—the smallest you should take—provides a margin of error of plus or minus 4.9 percent. Smaller samples increase the margin of error and limit your ability to look at the attitudes of subgroups in the population—like well-educated women or blue-collar men. I prefer samples of 800 because the margin of error is smaller and we get more accurate information about subgroups.

Expect to pay up to $10,000 for a comprehensive local issue survey, $15,000 for a regional issue, and $30,000 for a major, complex statewide issue. Costs also depend on how complex the issue is; the more complex, the more questions need to be asked. If you're going to have a total budget of over $100,000 for a local issue, you'll want to consider using a professional pollster.

If your budget is smaller than that, there are several ways to cuts costs by using volunteers. My colleague, Rick Claussen, used "the telephone book survey," in one low-budget campaign. To do this, you estimate the number of people in the telephone book you're going to use to get your voter sample. Divide that number by the number of interviews you need to complete. For instance, if you have 100,000 people in the phone book and you

POWER IN THE PEOPLE

want 1,000 interviews, you need to complete one survey for every hundred names in the book. So, you count down one hundred names and call that person. If there's no answer, call the next person. Keep calling down the list until you have completed a survey. Then count down one hundred names and start the process again.

Another option is to buy samples of registered voters from vendors. Or you may get some demographic balance by surveying people in places like grocery stores in different areas of your community.

You might also mix the following options and match them to your resources:

1. A professional pollster or volunteers design the survey.
2. Volunteers design the survey and a professional pollster reviews it.
3. A professional pollster or volunteers tabulate the survey data.
4. A professional pollster or volunteers interpret the tabulations and provide the analysis.
5. A local college class makes the survey a class project.

Having some guidance is better than guessing!

National or Local Pollster

If you use a professional, should you use a national or local pollster? It's natural to prefer working with people we know. Competence, however, is more important than where a pollster has offices or who the pollster's friends are. I've had wonderful successes working with Ernie Paicopolos of Opinion Dynamics, and Jan van Lohuizen of Voter Consumer Research, two of the best pollsters in the nation; my experience with local pollsters has been less satisfactory.

Committees are justifiably concerned about cost. But it isn't necessarily "you get what you pay for." National firms'

POLLING

costs are often competitive with local firms. Travel expenses don't need to be an issue. I've worked on low-budget campaigns where all the work was done by phone, fax and Federal Express. The client never met the pollster.

Process for Selecting a Pollster
Get references. Interview at least two pollsters. Ask them questions.
   1. *Does the pollster specialize on issues?* This is a very different field than either candidate or product marketing surveys?
   2. *How many issues has she or he polled on?* Of those issues, how many have been winners?

Ask to see some surveys they've designed.
   1. *Are the surveys comprehensive?*
   2. *Do they test a lot of messages?*
   3. *Do they ask the right questions?* On a property tax measure the committee based its decision to go to the ballot on the response to the question: Should the government buy greenspaces? Overwhelmingly people said yes. It was the wrong question! The question should have been: Are you willing to pay more property taxes to buy greenspaces?

The Pollster: Part of Your Team
Building teams is the most effective way of working in the world—and it's especially true of issue campaigns in election and non-election settings. On your strategy team, consider:
   1. Your pollster who will help identify your best messages and messengers;
   2. Your media consultant who will turn the pollster's findings in creative public communications;
   3. You and the Action Committee who will provide all the

POWER IN THE PEOPLE

background for the poll, ensure that all facts and figures are correct, check that the survey is balanced, and approve the final survey before it's fielded.

**Working together you build the solid foundation for a winning effort!
Making decisions together for the whole effort keeps everyone building the same house!**

7

MAKING A PLAN FOR ACTION

Know what you can control and what you can't.
Base your Action Plan on what you can control.

A campaign adage.

In small efforts—like getting a stop sign on your corner—the Action Plan can be a simple outline. For more complex efforts, like a statewide election, a comprehensive plan helps you stay focused and on schedule. In situations like the "Packwood matter," it's a "write-as-you-go" plan.

Action plans include sections on field analysis, strategies, communications, grassroots activities, budget/fund-raising, and a timeline.

FIELD ANALYSIS

What's involved in solving your issue? ASK!! If you want a stop sign, call your town or city government and ask what's involved in getting a stop sign. They may tell you how to succeed.

POWER IN THE PEOPLE

And there's where you start to draft your Action Plan. If it's a situation like the "Packwood matter," where there's no precedent, you'll have to start from the ground and build your plan.

STRATEGIES

You develop strategies by using information you already have: Your goal and which government you need to persuade. You ask questions:

1. *How can we persuade them?* By communicating with them.
2. *Who does the communicating?* Designated spokespersons determined by polling results, members of the Action Committee and its supporters through grassroots activities.
3. *How much will it cost to persuade them?* A realistic budget provides the answer.
4. *How will we raise the money to persuade them?* By a variety of fund-raising options.
5. *When do we need to persuade them?* That date and all the dates leading up to it are on your Timeline.

COMMUNICATIONS

The Plan's communications section answers these two general questions:

1. *To get the government action we want, who do we need to mobilize?* Neighbors? Opinion leaders? Special interest groups? The general public?
2. *What's the best way of mobilizing them?* At their front doors? Through their organizations? "Earned" media

MAKING A PLAN FOR ACTION

(there is no such thing as "free" media!) like news conferences and newspaper articles? Paid media—television, radio, newspaper? If you don't know, ask advice from people who have been successful communicating.

GRASSROOTS CAMPAIGN

You don't have a grassroots campaign without grassroots activities! The Plan's grassroots section answers these questions:
1. *Which traditional grassroots activities are appropriate for this issue? Will they work in your community?* Passing out information? Writing letters to the editor? Speaking to community organizations? Lobbying? Testifying at public hearings? Observing/monitoring government in action?
2. *Are there other activities that are used in your community?* Are they appropriate for this issue?
3. *Will you have the resources—volunteers, time, money—to do them effectively?*

BUDGET/FUND-RAISING

Have courage. Even successful professional managers and fund-raisers juggle numbers, make plans based on guesses, and revise the budget and fund-raising goals as they move through a project! But keep good records; you'll take some of the guess work out next time because you'll have a donor base, experience in event planning, and you'll know the rate of return and average size of contributions to expect from mailings.

The budget/fund-raising section answers four questions:
1. *How much money will we need?* It's smart to make two budgets: your big dream's budget and a rock-bottom budget.

POWER IN THE PEOPLE

Here are budget categories and items to get you started:

Overhead
Rent
Furniture/Equipment purchase
Furniture/Equipment rental
Phone installation
Phone & fax service
Equipment maintenance
Office maintenance
Office supplies
Printing
Postage/Shipping
Insurance
Security
Moving expenses
Bank charges
Travel/Mileage/Parking
Misc Expense/Petty Cash

Grassroots Campaign
Salaries, Unemployment & Taxes
    Director
    Support Staff
Materials design
    Brochures, flyers
Materials copying/printing
Speakers training
Speakers materials
Lobbying materials
Visual aids
Paraphernalia
    Bumper stickers
    Buttons
Shipping/postage
Travel/mileage

Paid Media
Media Consultant retainer
Radio/TV production
Radio/TV time
Print design
Print production
Print space
Outdoor advertising

Management Staff
Salaries, unemployment & taxes
    Manager
    Bookkeeper
    Support Staff
Travel/mileage

Fund-Raising
Salaries, Unemployment & Taxes
    Director
    Mail Coordinator
    Events Coordinator
    Support Staff
Printing
Postage/shipping
Events
Travel/mileage
Other

Phonebank
Salaries, unemployment & taxes
    Coordinator
    Support Staff
Materials preparation
Refreshments

Research
Pollster
Materials

Earned Media
Salaries, unemployment & taxes
    Media Relations Coordinator
Materials design
Materials copying/production
Visual aids
Clipping service
Media briefings
News conferences
Travel/mileage

Contingency

MAKING A PLAN FOR ACTION

My colleague, Rick Claussen, reminds me that, because "surprises" happen, we move ahead with the lower budget until we've got the funds we need for that. It's important, too, to get as much of the money in hand—or at least firmly committed—as early as possible so we can focus on what's important in issues: delivering messages. That's a lot easier when we're working with corporate clients than it is in citizen campaigns.

2. *How will we raise the money we need?* Options include Action Committee contributions and monthly pledges, mailing to lists you identified in the Resource Assessment; events; other fund-raising opportunities; personal mail or phone contacts with people and leaders of organizations; and, one-on-one meetings with potential generous "angels."

3. *When will we need the money?* Make a cash flow chart by week or month to show how much you'll need and when you'll need it. Seed money will come from your strongest supporters. In year-long, citizens' grassroots ballot measure campaigns as much as sixty percent of contributions come in the last eight weeks; it takes that long to get people's attention!

Here's one way to lay out a cash flow chart:

	Month 1	Month 2	Month 3	TOTAL
Pledges				
Mail				
Events				
Other Actv.				
Personal				
One-on-ones				
TOTAL				

POWER IN THE PEOPLE

See how short-term, achievable goals and creative thinking can lead to successful fund-raising.

Even so, it's important to make regular checks to see how close to the goal in each category you are. Based upon the checks, adjust the goals, and, if necessary, the budget.

4. *How much people power will we need to raise that much money in that time period?* It's obvious: Raising one hundred dollars takes far less organization and work than raising $1,000,000. Big budget citizens' grassroots campaigns need volunteers and a paid fund-raising team that may include a director, mail coordinator, events coordinator, and support staff.

Timeline/Master Calendar

A timeline/master calendar guides your decision-making process, defines your materials production schedule, and identifies your cash flow needs.

Whether you use a big wall calendar or a computer program, the process is the same. First, note dates on the calendar that could affect your efforts: holidays, school vacations, important community events. Next, enter key dates for your issue: public hearing and election dates, city council or school board meetings, contribution and expenditure reporting deadlines. Add dates for fund-raising events and drop dates for mailings. To show momentum building, have one week for bumper sticker distribution, the next week for putting out signs in businesses and supporters whose yards are on busy streets, and the last week or two for handing out campaign materials in high-visibility areas like shopping centers and sports event. Add other dates as they are scheduled.

MAKING A PLAN FOR ACTION

If possible, allow some "grace" time—city council meetings and elections dates are not flexible. You may have a little more control over public hearing dates.

Now go back and look at the Events Timeline in the Fundraising Chapter. That shows you how to layout your timeline.

PART

BUILDING PUBLIC SUPPORT
Putting Your Action Plan to Work

Now, it's time to put your **Plan for Action** into action. If you and other members of the Action Committee stay focused on your Plan, use your main messages every chance you get, are respectful of each other and people in your community, and follow the rules of the coalition, amazing things will happen! Some call it some good luck. It's really *planned* good luck.

Let's find out how to influence public opinion and create a political environment for the change you want by communicating your persuasive messages, getting editorial support, writing letters to the editor, and accepting speaking opportunities.

8

COMMUNICATING PERSUASIVE MESSAGES

Most voters want only enough information to know they're supporting a good cause and making an informed decision.

A campaign adage

Communicating political messages is not a recent phenomenon. The walls of Pompeii had political graffiti. Kites spread ancient Chinese slogans. Projectiles carrying messages behind enemy lines were used by our Revolutionary soldiers.

Modern technology has revolutionized communications making it more efficient and effective to reach masses of people located over the entire globe.

Without the national media, it's probable that the "Packwood matter" would have had a different ending. It was persistent, sensitive Florence Graves of *The Washington Post*, who broke the story. She deserves a Pulitzer Prize for her work! The national media—through news coverage, editorials, interviews, Murphy Brown, and Jay Leno—kept the story before the nation and especially before the Senate. The women who told

POWER IN THE PEOPLE

their stories of Senator Packwood's acts of sexual misconduct against them and those of us who worked on their behalf handled thousands of media calls. And we kept the issue alive by calling the media every time a new woman was ready to tell her story publicly or a different angle surfaced.

You have to know how to communicate your messages to get your story out. People's minds are cluttered with work, school, child care, church—you know the list—and important political issues like welfare and campaign finance reform. I read somewhere that people receive 2,500 messages a day. To have people "read" your message, you've got to cut through all that clutter so you . . .

REPEAT, REPEAT, REPEAT
YOUR ONE OR TWO MOST PERSUASIVE MESSAGES IN LANGUAGE THE GENERAL PUBLIC WILL UNDERSTAND!

Repeat your main message in your committee name, your logo, stationery and envelopes, every piece of campaign material, buttons and lapel stickers, the outside of fund-raising and information packets, the sign on the lectern at news conferences, in answers to questions. Use the same colors on all your materials. Every chance you get, repeat your main message.

Keep your messages simple. Remember the 1992 Clinton/Gore campaign message: "It's the economy, stupid."

Schedule your communications so you create a sense of momentum building. Tie your "earned communications" to paid media, if you're going to have it, and grassroots activities—phone banks, yard signs, bumper stickers, literature—so people get a sense of building to a climax and to victory.

Remember the persuasive, powerful messages you identified in your public opinion surveys? Let's organize and then see where and how to use them.

PERSUASIVE MESSAGES

ORGANIZING MEDIA CONTACTS

What newspapers, radio and television stations in your area are likely to cover your issue? Which reporters? What are their deadlines? To compile these ABCs of media contacts ask:

1. The local press club or state press association for a list, including names of reporters who specialize on your issue, publishers and editors, addresses, phone and fax numbers, and circulation of weekly and daily newspapers and special interest publications.
2. The local or state broadcasters association for a list of radio and commercial and cable television stations, names of reporters who specialize on your issue, station managers and owners, addresses, phone and fax numbers, size of audience, who their audience is (western, talk/news, Christian), and the names of communicasters and talk show hosts who would cover your issue.
3. A politically active friend, a political party, an organization you belong to, or a legislator who supports your issue for this information.

If you can't get the information any other way, then start with the Yellow Pages of your phone book.

You'll also need to know what, if any, position each of these media outlets has taken on your cause.

When you've got the information, you're ready to make a media contacts file. You do that by entering the information in a data base—it may take time, but is efficient for updating, making labels for mailing news releases and media advisories, keeping notes on your contacts and their reporting. As you get to know reporters, you'll want to exchange home phone numbers; You may need to talk about a late-breaking story after business hours. If you have access to a fax with a memory, you'll want to enter

POWER IN THE PEOPLE

the key fax numbers in the memory so you're ready to send out BULLETINS or news releases on a moment's notice.

In the clipping file, keep copies of every article and editorial on all sides of your issue. Always note the name of the paper, date of the article, the section, and place on the page where it appears. You may need this information as proof of bias if you find the other side is getting better coverage. File clippings in chronological order, the most recent clipping in front.

With your creativity, you'll find the information from clippings and electronic media invaluable. Here's how I used my clipping file in the early days of the "Packwood matter." The following are excerpts from a piece that was sent to United States Senators, national organizations, the media, and in fund-raising mailings to counter Packwood's claims that his troubles were politically motivated. The piece made clear that Packwood's misconduct was not only the concern of voters from a small western state; it was a politically powerful national issue.

" . . . reports of Packwood's behavior—which have not been denied by the Oregon Senator—depict a boorish and arrogant elected official who has manifested conduct unacceptable by any social standard . . . His alleged behavior is off the chart."
New York Post

"Sen. Bob Packwood's strategy of stonewalling charges of sexual harassment hasn't worked—and he knows it."
NEWSWEEK

"He used the power of his position for sexual purposes."
New York Times—editorial

"To hear a painfully long list of female ex-staffers tell it, he (Packwood) was privately pawing, smootching, patting, cornering, and otherwise hitting on women . . ."
Philadelphia Inquirer

PERSUASIVE MESSAGES

"The message the Packwood episode sends to Capitol Hill is that women are willing to risk humiliation or career damage by speaking out against sexual harassment"

TIME

MEDIA BRIEFINGS

After nearly three years of the "Packwood matter," one prime time television interviewer introduced "Senator Robert Packwood"; his name is "Bob." Other reporters continued to talk about "sexual harassment," a violation with which he was never charged. The Senate Ethics Committee found him guilty of "sexual misconduct," the much more serious crime of assault.

If the media doesn't get such basic facts correct, how can we know they get the substantive facts right? In fairness to the media, they're overworked, underpaid and expected to be experts on too many subjects.

They need you to help them get the facts of your cause straight. Remember the packets you put together for fund-raising calls? Prepare similar packets for reporters but include more "meaty" information. A summary of the proposed legislation and a copy of the full proposal. Scientific studies. Highlight key facts and figures. Your letterhead with a list of supporters and allies. A Q & A sheet with commonly asked questions and your answers. A map, graph, or drawing—help them visualize your facts.

Hold one-on-one meetings with key reporters and review the media packet with them. Or have a team of articulate experts make brief presentations during a continental breakfast for a group of reporters.

When a news report isn't accurate, call and tactfully point out the error to the reporter or send a copy of the clipping with your facts refuting the misinformation attached. Facts from third-party credible spokespersons will be more persuasive than "facts" that a reporter sees as political rhetoric. If the reporter

POWER IN THE PEOPLE

continues to report misinformation, see the head of the news department or the station owner. Layout your case clearly, firmly and politely. You can't afford to have voters misinformed about your issue. And you can't afford to antagonize the media. Remember the adage: It rarely makes sense to get in a battle of words with folks who buy ink by the barrel!

Whatever you do, in all the materials you pass out and in every answer, keep it "short and simple" and REPEAT, REPEAT, REPEAT your one or two best messages!

"Earned" Media

Some people call it "free media." There is no such thing! "Earned media" doesn't cost as much as paid media, but it can be expensive in other resources—and, you can't control the message. Most reporters give both sides of an issue; so by creating a news opportunity you've also created an opportunity for the other side. You must plan, prepare, strategize, be creative, develop effective materials, build good relationships with reporters and stay in regular contact with them.

Reporters cover your issue because they know you give them only newsworthy items and solid facts. You accommodate their deadlines, don't waste their time, make locations convenient for them and keep your issue on their desks and in their faces—in a nice way, of course.

"Earned media" is news coverage you get by creating news. Look at just one example of how my heroine, Alice Paul, used "earned media." She organized a coast-to-coast campaign tour that stopped in towns and cities all across the nation to collect signatures on a petition demanding women be allowed to vote. From San Francisco the group of three, colorful—perhaps even eccentric—women drove across the desert to Salt Lake City through sand "almost up to the running board," over the plains of

PERSUASIVE MESSAGES

Kansas, on to Chicago, and through the East—fording streams and enduring blizzards and miserable cold.

At every stop along the journey, Alice Paul's carefully selected colleague organized parades; dignitaries, governors, and mayors spoke; and people signed petitions. Reaching New York, the weather-beaten little car bearing the slogan ON TO CONGRESS and blazing "a path of purple and gold down the great thoroughfare," led a huge parade down Fifth Avenue.

In Washington, D.C., another huge parade led to the White House, where the women presented the President with their petition and its four miles of signatures.

In this historic adventure, Alice Paul used every "earned media" strategy available to her in 1915:

1. NEWS CONFERENCES
2. NEWS RELEASES
3. SPECIAL EVENTS
4. INTERVIEWS
5. OTHER OPPORTUNITIES

Today we add:
1. NEWS FEEDS
2. TECHNOLOGY OPTIONS

News Conferences

Stacy Pittman, the best media relations professional I've worked with, deserved the raves she got for arranging a one-day, seven-city "fly around Arkansas" news conference. The subject was the same in each city: AMENDMENT 6, IT'S A JOB KILLER! The media was alerted a week in advance with a media advisory giving details about the news conference—name and phone of contact person, purpose, day, time, place. They received

POWER IN THE PEOPLE

a fax reminder the day before the conference.

The "stars" were two University of Arkansas professors who discussed their economic analysis of the proposed measure. In each city, they used two thirty-inch by thirty-six-inch charts: one showed the predicted statewide job loses by industry segment; the other predicted local job losses. The television image of professors who looked like professors using charts with large, easy-to-read facts and figures reinforced our campaign's credibility and our message.

Media packets included prepared statements by the economists and a copy of their analysis.

The conferences were held at the airport in each city, so parking and the location were convenient for the media. A group of our supporters was at each spot and curiosity seekers made it look like we had a crowd. During the thirty-minute (they should never be longer) conference in each city, Stacy called key reporters in the next city to remind them of the time, place and importance of the subject. Her excellent strategy, careful planning (she even carried collapsible easels for the charts), personal contact, and hard work made this news conference a stunning success: It was covered by every television station and major paper in the state!

Here's a chart for arranging a news conference site—more of Stacy's good work.

PERSUASIVE MESSAGES

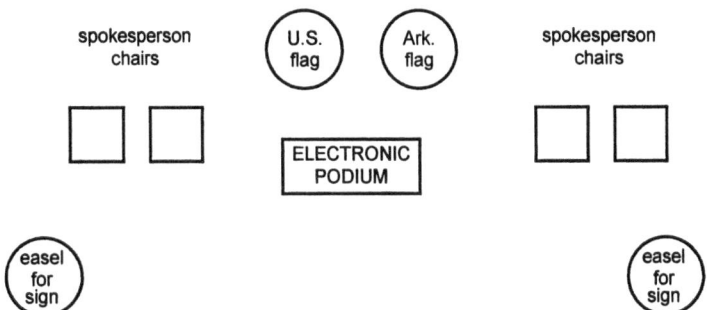

Row of 6 chairs—1st row reserved for media.
Row of 6 chairs—let media have chairs if needed.
Row of 6 chairs—for members of audience.

Let the crowd fill up the room behind the media and around the room.

TABLE	SMALLER TABLE
FOR LAPEL STICKERS, FOR AUDIENCE VOLUNTEERS TO SIGN, FOR WHITE INFORMATION PACKETS	MEDIA SIGN-IN SHEET, NEWS PACKETS (RED)

One potential downside to "earned media" is that reporters' pencils and editors' scissors control your messages. The best you can do is REPEAT, REPEAT, REPEAT your messages so reporters and editors have less to cut from.

News Releases

News releases are preferably one-page, one-and-one-half or double-spaced news stories printed on your committee letterhead. Here's a sample:

POWER IN THE PEOPLE

COMMITTEE TO SAVE ARKANSAS JOBS
506 Lyon Bldg., 401 W. Capitol
Little Rock, AR 72201   501/376-6151

NEWS RELEASE

October 14, 1994

FOR IMMEDIATE RELEASE

CONTACT: Stacy Pittman, 664-4411
Ed Smith, 534-0880

The following are remarks from Ed Smith, President of Smith Paper Company in Pine Bluff, Arkansas and one of 10,000 members of the Committee to Save Arkansas Jobs. His comments are regarding the Arkansas Supreme Court's ruling today to drop Amendment 6 from the November general election ballot.

"Justice has been served today by the Arkansas Supreme Court.

"The Committee to Save Arkansas Jobs has worked actively over the past months to inform voters that Amendment 6 was primarily an increased compensation package for trial lawyers. The Supreme Court affirmed that position.

"Amendment 6 would have been financially devastating for every Arkansan -- small business owners, school districts, hospitals, and taxpayers.

"Because of the misleading information voters received about Amendment 6, we're delighted that the measure has been removed from the general election ballot. However, we're confident that, had it gone to the ballot on November 8, Amendment 6 would have been overwhelmingly defeated."

Paid for by the Committee to Save Arkansas Jobs

The ingredients of a complete news release include:
1. RELEASE DATE giving day, date and time; or FOR IMMEDIATE RELEASE

PERSUASIVE MESSAGES

2. NAME OF CONTACT PERSON who can respond articulately to media inquiries
3. PHONE NUMBER where the contact person will be available
4. HEADLINE with strong language and in all caps
5. QUOTABLE QUOTES by credible spokespersons and experts
6. FACTS that are easily provable—too many facts confuse voters
7. INTERESTINGLY WRITTEN ANSWERS to who, when, why, what, where and how
8. YOUR ONE OR TWO BEST MESSAGES

It takes tight writing, but it's possible.

Put your most important information in the first paragraph. Have someone read the draft to check for correct statement of messages, facts and figures, grammar and spelling. Everything I write I read aloud to be sure it flows smoothly.

News Feeds

News feeds—sometimes called radio actualities—are messages that sound like newscasts. The feeds are recorded on a standard tape recorder and played over an answering machine. News feeds are a simple, inexpensive way to get your message out. Small radio stations are especially appreciative of news feeds—they help supplement limited news sources and resources. You can call radio stations to play the tape. When you "feed it, they're more likely to eat!" Or you can get an 800 number for them to call, which is what we did in Arkansas.

POWER IN THE PEOPLE

Here's an adaptation of information that was produced on NO on Amendment 6 committee letterhead and faxed to all radio stations in Arkansas. The actual feed had three sections; I've given you only two because of space limitations.

Following are two (2) actualities featuring Dr. Charles E. Venus, consulting economist and former economics professor at the University of Arkansas at Fayetteville.

Venus and Professor of Economics Dr. William P. Currington released today an economic impact study of the proposed constitutional amendment to restructure and revise the workers' compensation system in our state. Their data is based on a study released earlier by the National Council on Compensation Insurance. NCCI, a non-profit council, is the nation's largest workers' compensation statistical and data-gathering organization.

ACTUALITY #1

Announcer:
Two of Arkansas' renowned economists released an economic impact analysis of a proposal placed on the November ballot to restructure and revise the state's workers' compensation system. Dr. Charles Venus, one of the economists who conducted the study, discusses the projected job loss figures for Arkansas.

Venus:
The NCCI study concluded that 60,000 to 80,000 Arkansas jobs would be lost. Our analysis estimates that 70,000 jobs would be lost. That's almost 18,000 jobs in Arkansas' manufacturing sector and over 52,000 in the non-manufacturing sector that would be at risk. Naturally, Pulaski County will be the hardest hit since it's the state's most populated county.

PERSUASIVE MESSAGES

ACTUALITY #2

Announcer:
Drs. Venus and Currington also revealed economic data reflective of the proposal's impact on Arkansas taxpayers.

Venus:
State and local governments and the public schools are among the employers that must purchase workers' compensation insurance to cover possible injuries to their employees. We all know who funds the expenditures of the government . . . the taxpayer. Based on the current annual payroll of the state and local governments and public school employees, combined with a predicted one hundred percent increase in compensation costs, Arkansans can expect to see a seventy-two million dollar increase in taxes or reduced government and school services of equal value if the workers' compensation proposal passes.
If you have questions about this news feed or have problems with the toll-free number, please call Stacy Pittman at (501)664-4411

Special Events

In the 1991 pro-choice campaign in Washington state, we received good coverage for a unique event suggested by creative Tamar Abrams, Planned Parenthood Federation of America. We rented four cellular phones on a beautiful fall afternoon, the last Saturday before election day. "Call A Friend for Choice" signs at four different corners of Pike's Market drew people's attention. They were asked to call two friends—at our expense—to remind them to vote YES on 120 on Tuesday. We were reinforcing our message, had good visuals, and gave the media a different news angle for getting voters to vote.

In the 1992 Metropolitan Greenspaces Campaign, very short on money but strong in volunteers, we "Painted the Town Green." The media advisory had a tantalizing one liner: Next

POWER IN THE PEOPLE

Thursday everyone is going to be asking: What do all the green ribbons mean?

At 5 A.M. Thursday morning dozens of volunteers met and picked up assignments and bolts of two-and-one-half-inch bright green ribbon bought by a creative and ingenious volunteer, Bonnie Vawter, from a wholesale florist supplier. By the time commuters started for work, the Portland area was covered with thousands of green ribbons—lamp posts, trees, bridges, statues, car antennae, bicycles — the town was indeed painted green.

The question "What does the green mean?" was answered at a 10 A.M. news conference when representatives of supporting organizations gave brief statements to local media. That evening, headquarters was filled with environmentally oriented artwork and crowds drawn from people passing through Portland's gallery district on our monthly First Thursday. Donated wine and cheese were served as campaign workers "worked" the crowd with campaign information.

Over the weekend, there were walking trips to endangered greenspaces. Restaurants and businesses contributed 10 percent of their net proceeds to the campaign. The "Paint the Town Green" weekend took LOTS of work but we spread our message, created great media opportunities, had fun and made some green stuff, too. We lost the campaign, but planted the seeds for passage of a smaller bond measure two years later at a not-so-well-voted spring election.

INTERVIEWS

My first television interview came just after I became volunteer chair of the NO on 13 Campaign, the California proposition that started the national property tax revolt in 1978. A television crew came to interview me at home.

"Why should voters oppose Proposition 13?"

I was about sixty seconds into my ten-minute, League of

PERSUASIVE MESSAGES

Women Voters' speech—

"Cut! Lady, I got ten seconds, they got ten seconds and you got ten seconds. Now, why should voters oppose Proposition Thirteen?"

"Well, I don't know too much about taxes and government finance." What a stupid answer! Why in the world would the chairperson against a property tax measure say she didn't know anything about taxes and government finance?

My face was red and I was very embarrassed but I used that terrible experience to learn three lessons: Keep answers short. Keep answers simple. Be prepared.

You answer the phone. A reporter wants an interview NOW! Remember: You set your agenda. Explain politely that you can talk in fifteen minutes and ask what he or she wants to talk about. Now think very carefully: Who is the Action Committee spokesperson? Who has the facts? Is most articulate? Has credibility? You may decide to pass the call to someone else, but at least, talk with someone to be sure your message is right.

Whoever responds, the reporter must be called back in fifteen minutes. By then, the spokesperson will have practiced responses with someone else, checking that the responses are accurate and ten-to-fifteen seconds long. The spokesperson is cool, calm, has the facts and the cause's two main messages in mind.

Think of five hard questions a reporter might ask about your cause:

1._____
2._____
3._____
4._____
5._____

Now, write three sentence answers to each one. Be sure to end each answer with one of your cause's main messages.

POWER IN THE PEOPLE

Points to remember:
1. If the reporter asks a question you're not sure about, say so. But get them the answer ASAP!
2. Assume everything you say is on the record.
3. Be sure you understand the question before you give an answer.
4. Never say, "No comment."
5. Don't answer hypothetical questions.
6. Say only those things you'd like to see on the six o'clock news.
7. Don't be defensive, but don't assume the reporter is your friend.
8. Answer questions briefly, then move to your main messages.

Every interview is just another opportunity to REPEAT, REPEAT, REPEAT your main messages.

TECHNOLOGY OPTIONS

For someone of my generation who was in college before my family had television, all the new technology is mind boggling. I struggle to keep up with the changes, as most people do, but I'm learning: This book is being written on my laptop. You, too, need at least a working knowledge of the kinds of technology being used in political efforts today.

Within the last few years, the options for grassroots campaigns to communicate have expanded to 800 call-in numbers, alternative-media sources like C-SPAN and CNN, *Larry King Live*, *Geraldo*, talk radio, broadcast fax services, satellites, bulletin boards, the Internet, and E-mail.

PERSUASIVE MESSAGES

800 Numbers

In the Arkansas campaign, our television and radio spots offered people more information by calling our 800 number. Over 1,500 people called and within two days our office sent out the information they requested.

Because rates and services are changing so fast and vary from company to company I can't give you details and rates. Just call your long distance carrier for information. This important service may be easier and less expensive than you imagine and more effective than you dream.

Alternative-Media Sources

As with every other part of communicating, using alternative-media sources such as C-SPAN and CNN; *Larry King Live*; *Geraldo*; and talk radio, takes your initiative and tenacity—unless you're working on something like the "Packwood matter." When there were rumors in Washington, our phones rang off the hook. One morning, I had twenty-two calls from national media!

For either local or national television or radio shows, contact the station directly. They'll want to know why your story is news worthy, who the spokesperson will be, what her or his credentials are, and when the timing is right. Major shows require written request. Send it. Be persistent. You might eventually connect with the right person, the station's programming may need your kind of story, or the timing of other issues might make them more receptive to your issue. Keep calling until they say, "WE'RE NOT INTERESTED!"

Broadcast Fax Services

Now here's an amazing service! It's a simple, fast and inexpensive communications technique without the cost to you of equipment, installation, extra phone lines and staff time.

You provide your list to a vendor and give instructions on where and when you want your materials faxed. The vendor does the rest.

POWER IN THE PEOPLE

Another option to arrange through the same vendor is called "InfoFax." This service is great for updates, media, fundraising, action alerts, coalition updates, and reports. Once your fax directory is stored, you can send information over your phone by fax twenty-four hours a day, seven days a week. Your list is protected with a password, so only people you authorize can use the service.

The Florida Chamber of Commerce used its state-of-the-art broadcast fax with terrific results. The Chamber was notified that the Florida Department of Labor was proposing a rule that companies would be fined if their employees lifted more than fifty-one pounds—a rule that would be devastating for many businesses. The Chamber faxed all 12,000 of their members asking if the rule would cause their businesses problems. Members were told their fax responses would be photocopied on red paper and taped together to form a "giant ribbon of red tape."

Media updates were issued as responses rolled in. First the ribbon of red tape was as tall as a twenty-two story building; then as tall as the Empire State Building. At its last measurement, the red tape was more than one-third of a mile long. That's a lot of red tape!

Satellites

The use of a satellite saved me almost $10,000! Political spots produced in Los Angeles were sent by air courier to me in Omaha for a focus group that night. Unfortunately, the tape was never found after it left LA. But arrangements for the focus groups were completed. My options were to cancel the groups—and still pay $10,000 for the completed arrangements, reschedule the groups which wouldn't give me the information I needed to make critical decisions, or have the spots sent by satellite for a cost of $900. Within thirty minutes after the arrangements were made, I had my spots in Omaha!

Satellites are useful, too, for interactive meetings which

PERSUASIVE MESSAGES

allow people in different locations to see and hear the other speakers and audience at the same time.

For information on arranging to use satellites contact a satellite broker. Your local television station can help you find one.

Bulletin Boards, the Internet, and E-Mail

The development and quick acceptance of The Internet and other information services by the general public is rapidly changing the way we communicate. As more and more people take advantage of this Star Wars technology, fewer and fewer people depend on traditional media to communicate their views. Soon, for example, reporters and columnists will "self publish" their work instead of relying on a newspaper, magazine, station or network to send their views to an audience. Reporters will reach their audience directly.

You can use this technology now to help your cause in several ways.

1. You can discuss your issue with like-minded folks through existing "bulletin boards" and "forums" using information services like CompuServe and America On-Line.
2. You can create a forum for discussion and invite others to join.
3. If there is sufficient interest, you can schedule specific on-line "conferences" or "chat rooms" to focus discussion of the issue.

Check with your information service for instructions. They want your business and will be glad to advise you on the best use of their service.

Many groups and companies use The Internet's World Wide Web to create a "Home Page." This is a comprehensive resource for web users that gives them everything they ever

POWER IN THE PEOPLE

wanted to know about you and your issue. You can use "Home Page" for things like exploring the history of your issue, facts and figures, background information, notes and quotes, requests for contributions, campaign plans, how you can help, etc. You can even store graphic images, such as your logo, that users can download for their own use!

Some of these computer services are expensive and most require a fairly sophisticated understanding of computer technology and programming. If you, like me, are not a high-tech kind of person, don't despair! Start low tech—with a phone book. Talk with your friends and associates for a recommendation on a competent computer consultant, get some leads from the phone book, check their references, understand the costs involved and then just do it!

I don't know the technology of how it happens, but I know that if I strike a match in a certain way, it will ignite; and if I carefully put the match next to the wick of a candle, I'll be able to see in the dark! Don't be intimidated as I was until my dear friend and team captain, Frank Schubert, helped me over a mental mountain. Focus on using the technology for what you do understand—communicating the merits of your issue.

OTHER EARNED MEDIA OPPORTUNITIES

Other opportunities for "earned media" are limitless. Rallies. Parties. Races. Announcement of a new major endorser. Passage of a resolution by a prominent civic club. A celebrity event. Presentation of a petition. An important announcement. A human face on your issue in a feature news story. A correction when opposition facts and figures are wrong. CAUTION: On this last idea, be sure you don't look nit-picky or petty. Just set the record straight.

Here are some suggestions on collecting signatures:

PERSUASIVE MESSAGES

Have petitions available at all of your meetings and as part of your regular routine:
- Circulate petitions on clipboards through the audience during lectures and seminars, or have one available in your waiting room at all times.
- Have a table set up in lobbies, waiting rooms for petition signing.
- Ask everyone who comes into your meeting hall or office to sign a petition and to take one home to gather signatures of friends and family.

Encourage your professional colleagues to join the petition campaign:
- Contact professionals at organizations and institutions related to your cause.
- Encourage them to collect signatures.

Reminder: Get a signature, printed name, and address from each person. Invite people to write a personal message in addition to signing their name.

To be effective any of these opportunities must follow the same guidelines for effective "earned media": Reinforce your main messages, don't compete with other big news stories, be news worthy, and VERY VISUAL—one picture is worth 1,000 words. Use your imagination. Have fun—if it's appropriate for your cause.

PAID ADVERTISING

For the stop-sign-on-your-corner campaign, you don't need paid advertising. For that kind of cause good organization, word-of-mouth, "earned media," neighborhood coffees, and campaign materials delivered door-to-door will communicate your messages.

POWER IN THE PEOPLE

For major, statewide ballot measures on contested, controversial issues you can't win without paid advertising!

Effective paid advertising makes people aware of issues and persuades undecideds. Budget, region and issue will determine what combination of paid mediums you'll use: television, radio, newspaper or outdoor/collateral materials like brochures, bumper stickers, lawn signs.

Television

If you can raise the money, television should be your first priority. According to political science professor Russ Dondero, 70 percent of voters get most, if not all, voting information from television, primarily from political ads!

Television is the most powerful, cost-effective medium because it reaches the most people per dollar spent. It has visual impact, highlights your message with color, allows you to put words on the screen as a spokesperson gives facts so viewers get a double wham of your message. It moves people emotionally. It makes your main messages clear and easy for people to remember.

Community access cable has become an important means of talking among neighbors and is something you'll want to consider.

Radio

Radio is inexpensive to produce and place, easy to control production quality of, and is especially good to supplement television. In fact, radio ads are often lifted right off the sound tracks of television spots. In certain situations, radio is the medium of choice. If limited budget removes television as an option, radio allows you to talk to people. Radio makes it easy to target audiences. It's especially good for drive time in areas where people you want to talk to commute.

PERSUASIVE MESSAGES

Newspaper

Print—daily, weekly community and entertainment papers, and tabloids—is normally thought to be the least effective of paid advertising choices, but it has its place. It can support other mediums or it can stand alone. It's a cost-effective way of telling people in your community about your issue. If you're in a major media market but need to talk with people in only a small part of the market, use the zoned edition of papers and you'll pay only to reach the people who need to know about your issue. Sometimes we use print to deliver our messages to opinion leaders and readers who often are people who want more information than we can put in a thirty second television or radio commercial.

Production

Production of paid advertising, especially television and radio, is one thing few grassroots groups have the experience or expertise to do effectively. Writing a script that is clear, makes a credible statement, stands out from media clutter, and keeps the main message simple is very hard! Creating a set, getting good lighting and sound quality, working with talent—paid or unpaid—following union regulations and labor laws require experienced professionals.

People are often shocked when my Emmy-award-winning colleague, Ben Goddard, a crew of eight to ten specialists, and I work a tough eight hours to get one thirty second spot. Every detail must be perfect. One glitch in a thirty second spot means people miss the message. The best concept in the world won't work if it isn't high production quality. It won't grab people's attention. It'll get lost in their clutter and an opportunity and money are wasted.

I like thirty second spots better than longer spots. As with direct mail, the shorter the message the more focused and clear it is. And, if I air two thirty second spots instead of one sixty sec-

POWER IN THE PEOPLE

ond (at little more cost), I'm following the adage: REPEAT, REPEAT, REPEAT the message!

In the 1991 Washington state pro-choice campaign, David Mitchell produced a ten second spot and a thirty second spot. In that campaign, the ballot language was so confusing that polls showed nearly 25 percent of the people who said they would vote NO, in fact, wanted to vote pro-choice; that meant they had to vote YES. The ten-second spot used the close of the thirty-second spot. There were words on the screen while the announcer voice-over said: Vote Pro-choice. Planned Parenthood and the League of Women Voters urge you to vote YES 120. Pro-choice. It was a great strategy. And especially effective given the handicap of terrible ballot language, voter confusion on the language, a well-funded opposition and our limited funds.

To find a professional for television and radio production, it's good business practice to send requests for proposals (RFPs) to several media consultants. Ask them:

1. What issue campaigns they've worked on;
2. How many they've won;
3. Review a reel of their spots. When reviewing spots, look for clear presentation of messages. Creative, clever, artistic spots can look good but they may detract from the message. Viewers may be so taken with the beauty or cleverness, they miss the message.

In 1980, I wrote a television script titled "Roller Coaster" for an electric utility client. Oil shortages. Price hikes. More shortages. Oil surpluses. It was filmed on the roller coaster at Magic Mountain. The client loved the spot. We were thrilled with it. So thrilled, in fact, that the same spot was filmed at Coney Island for another client. As we do with spots, we did a poll before and a poll after the spots ran. Result: NO MOVEMENT! It was a creative, dramatic ad but it didn't do the job.

PERSUASIVE MESSAGES

4. Be very clear about your budget limitations. Be sure you have a contract that says how many spots you will receive for a specific dollar amount. A true professional will find ways to keep production costs within your budget;

5. Get references and call them!

Whoever does your production, be sure to have written documentation proving the facts you use. Some stations demand documentation before they'll air political spots. In other instances, your opposition may try to get stations and papers to refuse to place your advertising by challenging your statements. This documentation could be good in media packets, too.

Closed Captioning

To add your voice to the call for a more humane, inclusive society and to get your messages to as many people as possible, consider having your television spots closed captioned. It's as easy as sending your master tape and a script to the National Captioning Institute at 703/917-7600 or 818/238-0068.

Placement

Placement of paid advertising, too, is a job for professionals. They have computer data that selects what programs reach your target audiences, how many times you have to run a spot to break through the public's clutter. They know how to negotiate rates. Ask your media consultant for a recommendation.

9

GETTING EDITORIAL SUPPORT

Success usually accompanies attention to little details.

John Wooden,
legendary coach who led the UCLA men's
basketball teams to ten NCAA championships

Editorial endorsements are important to candidates; they're vital to issue causes and campaigns. With a candidate you have political stands, energy, party affiliations, organization alliances, personality and family values to move the public. With an issue you have no soul. No human dynamics. You have only an idea to sell.

Citizens look to editorials to help them make their own decisions on issues. They want to know, especially on complex, controversial issues, who supports and who opposes them. Editorials give your position credible, third-party endorsements. And they send a message: It's socially acceptable to take this position.

POWER IN THE PEOPLE

In the 1990 Oregon pro-choice campaign, the campaign that established my national reputation, every major paper in the state editorialized against the ban on abortions and, to the amazement of most people, the majority editorialized against the parent notice measure. How did we do it?

We used teams. For each community we put together a team of local, community leaders who could speak credibly about the main points of our issue: religious, medical, legal, and the campaign itself.

On the Portland team, for example, where we met with the editorial board of The Oregonian, the largest, most influential daily paper in the state, we included:

1. A minister. The Bishop of the Oregon Conference of the United Methodist Church discussed the ethical and moral issues of abortion on behalf of the major, mainline denominations who support a woman's right to choose.
2. A physician. The past president of the Oregon Medical Association, who did his medical school residency in obstetrics and gynecology before Roe versus Wade, discussed the health consequences of not having legal abortions available.
3. A lawyer. The president of the board of our local Planned Parenthood discussed the legal inadequacies of the ballot measures we were working to defeat.
4. Campaign staff. As campaign manager, I answered questions about the campaign and made sure our campaign messages were REPEATED, REPEATED, AND REPEATED.

We prepared well. Because team members were very busy people, we spent just fifteen minutes together before the meeting. I gave each of them a card with the two simple, key points it would be logical for them to make. Our main message was printed in red letters at the bottom of the card. My goal is to have messages repeated at least ten times in an hour meeting. You think

GETTING EDITORIAL SUPPORT

that's overkill? Martin Luther King, Jr., said, "I have a dream," eleven times in two minutes.

We handed out information. Each member of the editorial board was given a copy of our media information packet so they had all of our facts and figures in writing. This technique helps cut down on inaccurate reporting.

Because our teams across the state REPEATED, REPEATED, AND REPEATED our campaign messages, the editorials streamed in using our messages as their rationale for taking our side. We picked key headlines and sentences from a variety of papers so voters saw our statewide support in major city daily and weekly papers in rural communities. And we used selected headlines and sentences in all communications—television, radio, flyers. The result: Voters got our messages over and over again in every part of the state from one of the major influences on issues: local newspapers.

Put your "dream team" together. To do it, look at your issue. What are its main points? Who is the leading voice on each of these points?

MAIN POINTS	LEADING VOICES
_____	_____
_____	_____
_____	_____
_____	_____

Now think: Do these people show the diversity of my community? Is there some angle that could make the issue more appealing to the specific paper we're talking to? Are the people on my list willing to work with me and take suggestions? On the basis of your answers, make adjustments to your list of LEADING VOICES.

You've just identified the members of your editorial-meeting team and what each one should talk about. That's important in recruiting, because you give these spokespersons confidence

POWER IN THE PEOPLE

that they only have to talk about the part of your cause dealing with their expertise.

Now recruit your team and help them prepare to get editorial endorsements. One of the most rewarding times of issues' efforts is watching the editorials come in with your messages. When that happens you know you've done your job very well!

10

LETTERS TO THE EDITOR

Fortune cookie:

Great thoughts come from the heart.

So do letters to the editor. And they have facts—so they come from your head, too. The heart and the head messages are so important because you'll be telling the largest audience you'll probably ever talk to about your important issue or campaign. You want readers to feel some emotion or empathy for the people who are affected by the issue; people respond when they feel emotional. And you need to give them one or two facts so you appeal to their intellect, too.

A good way to estimate how many people may read your letter to the editor is to simply divide the circulation of your local paper in half. That number tells you why it's important to learn how to write letters to the editor that get printed!

Look what a systematic, coordinated letters-to-the-editor campaign achieves:

POWER IN THE PEOPLE

1. *You reenforce your most important message*—that's for all the readers;
2. *You give readers one or two other messages* that are consistent with your main message and that will appeal to a specific demographic group;
3. *People other than your primary spokesperson give the messages* so readers learn that lots of people from different walks of life and parts of your community care about the issue;
4. *You increase the number of people who have facts about your issue*; and
5. *With these facts, others may be inspired to join with you.*

"Effective" is the key word. In the case of letters to the editor, it isn't people's personal clutter you have to cut through; it's the clutter on the editor's desk. *The New York Times* gets about 1,500 letters a week and prints sixty; *Time* magazine gets about 1,500 and prints thirty-five, according to J. Peter Zane, of *The New York Times*. Local papers, too, print far fewer letters than they receive.

Here's how you make this "earned" media technique work for your cause:

1. *Write the letter so it's easy to read.* Double-spaced, typed letters are preferred.
2. *Keep letters short and simple.* Two or three paragraphs are enough. Many publications insist that letters contain no more than 250 words. Longer letters are likely to be edited or not printed at all; and if they're printed, less likely to be read.
3. *Put your most important statement in the first sentence or two.*
4. *Use an experience to make your letter more personal.* That's where the heart of your story comes in.

LETTERS TO THE EDITOR

5. Include one or two facts—so your letter appeals to readers' "heads."
6. The salutation should be: *To the Editor*:
7. The closing should be: *Sincerely,*
8. *Put your name, street address and daytime phone number under your signature.* The paper won't print this last information, but needs it for identification and confirmation purposes.
9. If you're writing to more than one paper, *send each paper an original, not a copy, of the same letter.*
10. *Relate your letter to a previous story,* editorial, ad or other letter; it's likely to be published sooner.

You'll encourage others to write letters to the editor about your cause if you give them one or two key points to include in their letters or if you give them sample letters. In the Arkansas ballot measure campaign, for example, we wrote sample letters that might be sent by a farmer, hospital administrator, small business owner, or poultry farmer. Here's the poultry farmer's sample letter:

To the Editor:

The poultry industry creates one out of every twelve jobs in our state—and keeps thousands of people on their family farms. Providing Amendment 6's enormous costs of workers' compensation for all these employees would devastate family farmers and our state's economy.

Amendment 6 must be defeated.

Sincerely,

(your name)
(your address)
(your phone)

POWER IN THE PEOPLE

How did we put "heart" in this letter? And "head?"

To get your thinking started, name two demographic groups who support your issue and one or two points that would be especially persuasive to them.

GROUP   MESSAGES
_____   _____
_____   _____

Now write a sample letter to the editor for each group. Do they each come from your "heart" and have some "head" in them, too?

11

SPEAKING OPPORTUNITIES

The Book of Lists:

The average American's biggest fear is public speaking.

It need not be so. People who know me now don't believe it when I tell them that as I was coming out of my cocoon in the late-sixties, public speaking for me was such a traumatic experience, I vomited! Had nightmares. Gasped for breath. But I knew if I walked to the edge I'd land on something solid. So I just kept trying, with the result that I've spoken to audiences of up to 1,000 people with only the adrenaline rush that comes from doing something exciting. It beats sky diving!

How did I learn? I practiced; listened to myself on tape; watched myself on video; learned from my screw ups; and I had the opportunity to observe Michael Sheehan, who prepares presidential candidates for speeches and debates, work with others.

POWER IN THE PEOPLE

LESSONS I'VE LEARNED
1. *Make an outline* of the five or six points I want to talk about.
2. *Use a personal story* to show why the issue is important.
3. *Keep it simple!* Make points conversational and "listener friendly," rather than academic and boring.
4. *Keep it short!* Talks on issues to civic clubs can be as short as ten minutes; if they're longer, I'm probably giving more information than the audience wants or needs.
5. *Talk my talk* in the shower and on the way to the meeting so that I'm completely familiar with the material.
6. *Before a speech to a large audience, check out the room, stand at the podium, visualize the people, adjust the height of the microphone, say several sentences over the sound system.*
7. *Know the audience.*
8. *Wear professional but comfortable clothes and shoes*, put a hankie and reading glasses in a pocket, make a last minute mirror check to be sure I look as good as I can and then forget about looks.
9. *Arrive early and make new friends.*
10. *Give two of these new friends each a question to ask, so the Q & A gets off to a fast start.*
11. As I'm being introduced, *I breathe deeply.*
12. *Have a glass of water handy.*
13. *Appreciate the opportunity* to tell people about an important issue.
14. *Make eye contact* with new friends and talk to them from my heart. Once I feel comfortable, I speak to others in the audience.
15. *Use a few facts and third-party quotes* to support the position.

SPEAKING OPPORTUNITIES

16. If there's a question and answer time, *prepare two or three sentence answers to tough questions* and say them out loud.
17. When talking on a controversial issue, I *plan a strategy for defusing anger.*
18. I *Avoid equipment and charts* unless I'm absolutely sure the equipment will work and everyone in the audience can easily read the charts.
19. *Don't argue* with someone whose mind I'm not going to change.
20. REPEAT, REPEAT AND REPEAT the main messages in the talk and responses to questions.
21. *Pass out materials at the end* of the talk so people aren't reading them while I'm talking.

In addition to these specific lessons, I've developed a philosophy about speaking. People learn better when they're interacting with one another. Audiences learn more when the person in front *talks with* them rather than *speaks at* them. I read somewhere that people's attention span is about two-and-one-half minutes. If that's true, and I talk for thirty minutes, the audience hasn't heard most of what I've said. That's why I like ten-minute talks and twenty minutes for answering questions. The audience gets the same amount of information as if I speak for thirty minutes.

The audience isn't going to remember what I've talked about if they're glassy-eyed with boredom. If I give the audience only some information, they'll ask questions. Then I know I'm giving them the information they're interested in having, rather than my making an assumption about what they want to know.

WHERE TO SPEAK

Action Committees must actively seek speaking opportunities—as long as they're before friendly or at least non-hostile

POWER IN THE PEOPLE

audiences. Once you have a corps of trained speakers, seek out places for them to speak. Remember the long list of groups we looked at to find Action Committee members? Go back to that list to find audiences for speakers. Call them and offer a speaker for a general meeting.

DEBATES

There are few circumstances where it's wise to participate in a debate on an issue.

In my experience, the supporting and opposing groups turn their members out in full force for debates; there are seldom undecided or swing voters in the audience. Too often someone becomes rude. The media, rather than talking about the facts of the issue, reports on a more "sexy" news angle: confrontation. It's a losing situation for everyone, especially anyone in the audience who gets turned off by adversaries shouting at one another.

When asked to debate, offer other options. Explain you'd like to be part of the program but you think the audience will get better information if the two sides speak at different programs. A second option is for both sides to speak at the same program for a specific time limit and then respond to written questions only. In either case, you'd like to speak last.

Allowing only written questions makes the best use of the audience's time; people don't have the opportunity to make long statements before they get to their questions. The audience, after all, has come to hear you, not the group's members, speak.

There are times when, for public relations reasons, you must participate in a debate. Here in Portland, Oregon, for instance, there's a six o'clock Sunday evening Town Hall that gets about one-third of the viewing audience. Saying "no" isn't an option. Instead, we do the same type of preparation we do for editorial board visits. We carefully select who represents our side, give each of them a cue card with the two points he or she should make and a key message written on the bottom of the card.

SPEAKING OPPORTUNITIES

PREPARING A TEAM OF SPEAKERS

I like to work with four or five potential committee speakers for a three-hour session. I use about twenty minutes to discuss techniques for talking about issues, to explain how we developed the cause's messages, and the importance of sticking to those messages. We review the sample speech for about ten minutes. The rest of the time is spent answering tough questions. The more time speakers spend practicing, the more likely they are to REPEAT, REPEAT, REPEAT the messages.

When we did speakers' coaching with key spokespersons in the 1994 Arkansas campaign, one wonderful man just didn't get the concept of short answers and ending with our messages. After about twenty minutes of drilling him and critiquing his performance, he stopped in the middle of a very long answer and said, "No, what I'm supposed to say is 'Amendment 6 is a job killer.'" Everyone clapped for his success.

Speakers' manuals include:

1. A brochure or fact sheet
2. A list of supporters
3. Basic information about the issue
4. A draft speech
5. A sample speech outline
6. Key points and facts in several places in the manual to reenforce the REPEAT, REPEAT, REPEAT technique
7. Tough questions and suggested answers
8. Supporting documentation

BE PREPARED

Here's information for speakers to confirm:

1. Date, day and time of the talk
2. Place, directions to the location, and parking information

POWER IN THE PEOPLE

3. Who is the audience, their knowledge of and interest in the issue
4. Format of the program
5. Other participants
6. Length of time for the talk. Suggest you'd like to talk for about ten minutes.
7. Length of time for questions
8. The club policy on passing out information and asking for contributions.

Here's a list of things for speakers to take to pass out:

1. Brochures or fact sheets, a list of supporters, etc.
2. Volunteer sign-up cards
3. Contribution cards and envelopes
4. Bumper stickers and buttons

ANSWERING QUESTIONS

Michael Sheehan, the guru of media trainers, developed a "touch-and-go" strategy for responding to questions: You "touch" on the answer to the question and "go" with your message. I have a more precise guideline: Use one sentence to answer the question and two sentences for your message.

I did an hour-long talk show on Wisconsin Public Radio on the subject of public hearings on the "Packwood matter." This interview was after Senator Barbara Boxer's motion for public hearings was defeated. At the time our three main messages were:

1. Senator Packwood's misconduct;
2. The "Packwood matter" wasn't a partisan issue;
3. The failure to hold public hearings broke Senate Ethics Committee precedent.

SPEAKING OPPORTUNITIES

Here are edited excerpts from that interview:

WPR. What would be served by public hearings?

J.F. This is the first time in the history of the Senate Ethics Committee when "substantial credible evidence" has not led to public hearings. This breaks precedent with the procedures of the Ethics Committee by not having public hearings.

WPR. Here are a couple of paragraphs from *The New York Times*: Senator McConnell said the Boxer Resolution would mark "the end of the Ethics process" in which a bipartisan panel equally divided could do its work without interference. Permitting intervention by the full Senate, he said, would allow the Committee to be "treated like a political football propelled in any direction the majority seeks to push it." There would be "a return of the bad old days," he warned, where we would deal with misconduct on a partisan basis. Isn't there that danger with public hearings?

J.F. That's news coverage. But a *(The) New York Times* editorial said, "All Senator Boxer was trying to do was require the committee to follow its own longstanding procedure of holding open hearings in major ethics cases." There are numerous other editorials across the nation calling for public hearings. A Gannett newspaper editorial said, ". . . there is a matter of precedent. If the Senate is guided by history, the hearings will be held." *The Idaho Statesman* said, ". . . Senator Bob Packwood's fellow club members in the U.S. Senate closed ranks, preferring to protect his interests over those of the American public." *The Oregonian* said, "Hearings have

POWER IN THE PEOPLE

been, all along, the best route for airing the complete Packwood case."

WPR. But the issue is open hearings or not.

J.F. The issue is whether the Senate will act in a way that says to women across the nation that senators have heard these serious charges and that the women who had the courage to come forward will not be ignored.

WPR. The question is why do we need to do this in the public eye?

J.F. Why don't we? Why should the "Packwood matter" break Senate precedent? Because the charges are so embarrassing? Does that mean the more embarrassing the charges against a senator, the less likely the Senate will stick to its precedent?

WPR. Because the decision won't be made on the basis of rational judgement of the Ethics Committee. The decision becomes this political football.

J.F. The Senate Ethics Committee precedent is to hold public hearings. Only in the "Packwood matter" has the concern about political football been more important than the precedent.

WPR. There isn't any secrecy about these charges. I think you might be able to make the case that there's more likely to be appropriate punishment doled out without public hearings if the issues weren't dealt with adequately. Know what I mean?

SPEAKING OPPORTUNITIES

J.F. I do know what you mean. On the other hand the Senate Ethics Committee has met with Bob Packwood. They have heard his side of the story from him. They have not met with the women. Only the Senate Ethics Committee staff has met with the women. We believe there is a lot of difference between meeting one-on-one, eyeball-to-eyeball in a discussion about a person's sexual misconduct and reading off a piece of paper. You have no sense until you've met these women about their credibility, their sincerity, their integrity. You don't get that off a piece of paper.

W.P.R. So the Ethics Committee has *not* met with these women?

J.F. That's right. In Senate Ethics Committee precedent, that's the purpose of public hearings.

W.P.R. I'm sure a lot of the Democrats who voted for public hearings were less interested in justice being done to this Senator than they were in the political advantage that the Democrats could have gained from public hearings.

J.F. Well, people can say that. But remember, we know of two votes that the Senate Ethics Committee has taken. Both of them were six to zero. The first vote was in October 1993 on whether to ask the full Senate for authorization to subpoena Packwood's diaries. That vote was six to zero. And the vote by the full Senate was ninety-four to six giving the Committee the authority to subpoena. The second six to zero vote—again three Republicans and three Democrats—was in May of this year when the Committee passed its five-page resolution listing the "substantial credible evidence" of Packwood's sexual misconduct, altering of evidence, and improperly

POWER IN THE PEOPLE

asking for financial favors from people who do business before Packwood's committees.

The "Packwood matter" isn't a partisan issue.

WPR. There are other people in high places in Washington who have records of sexual misconduct, even murder. Let's have public hearings on all of them.

J.F. This discussion is about Senator Packwood's conduct. We need to stay focused on the Ethics Committee findings of "substantial credible evidence" that Senator Packwood committed acts of sexual misconduct against seventeen women, "intentionally altered his diaries," and "solicited or otherwise encouraged offers of financial assistance from persons who had a particular interest in legislation or issues that Senator Packwood could influence."

WPR. But why do we need public hearings?

J.F. Bob Packwood, until this late date, has himself called for public hearings. He did it in 1992. He did it in 1993. And he did it again in 1994. He has said, "We need to have an open hearing so I can question those persons who wish to hide anonymously making statements about my conduct and expose their contradictions in the harsh light of an open forum. So I can question those people who don't have the guts to confront me in the public eye."

WPR. Your point is that Republicans don't want public hearings and Democrats do.

J.F. My point is that this is not a partisan issue. Many of the

SPEAKING OPPORTUNITIES

women who have come forward with their stories were on Packwood's staff. They were his loyal supporters. They were campaign workers who worked in volunteer situations. One of them, a seventeen-year-old, was an intern on his staff and a baby sitter for the Packwood children.

WPR. But the man isn't guilty of anything yet.

J.F. The Senate Ethics Committee, after a thirty-one-month investigation, has found "substantial credible evidence" that he has committed acts of sexual misconduct against seventeen women, "intentionally altered his diaries," and "solicited or otherwise encouraged offers of financial assistance from persons who had a particular interest in legislation or issues that Senator Packwood could influence."

WPR. Is there a general political case you want to make that's over and above Packwood's political problems?

J.F. This is the issue: Is the Senate going to deal openly with sexual misconduct as they do with every other situation, or is there going to be a continuation of sweeping it under the rug and hoping that people will forget about it.

WPR. I'm not from Oregon, but what can I do to help?

J.F. Thank you very, very much for your support. Three things come to mind. Number one, you can congratulate your two Senators for their votes for open hearings. You can watch closely during these next few weeks to see how things unfold and then let the Ethics Committee know what you think. And number three, you can send

POWER IN THE PEOPLE

us a contribution. The work we've done over the last thirty-one months is expensive.

WPR. An individual is not guilty until proven guilty. Mr. Packwood is entitled to due process. And due process is to let the Ethics Committee do its work.

J.F. We absolutely agree with you. And in this case, as in all others the Ethics Committee has handled, requires public hearings now that "substantial credible evidence" of serious wrong doing has been found.

WPR. Mr. Packwood may or may not be guilty, but he's entitled to due process just like anyone else. We don't know what's true and what's not true. That's what the Committee is for.

J.F. I absolutely agree with you and believe in due process. And due process in the tradition and precedent of the Senate Ethics Committee is to hold public hearings. We are simply asking that the precedent be followed.

WPR. It always seems as though when it's Republican that it's not public.

J.F. I don't think there should exceptions for anybody. I don't care what their party is. The issue is their conduct.

WPR. I don't think Bob Packwood ought to have another forum to parade his activities around in. I just don't see any benefit.

J.F. You and I disagree. Let's go back to the real issue. The real issue is Senator Packwood's behavior as described in

SPEAKING OPPORTUNITIES

the five-page resolution passed unanimously—three Republicans and three Democrats—citing acts of sexual misconduct against seventeen women, altering of documents and obstructing the investigation by tampering with evidence.

WPR. Public hearings don't serve the public interest and doesn't use our taxpayer very wisely.

J.F. A recent CBS-(*The*) *New York Times* poll shows that sixty percent of Americans want public hearings. Men are equally as likely as women to want public hearings about Packwood. Fifty-seven percent of Republicans and seventy percent of those eighteen to twenty-nine years old want public hearings.

WPR. I don't believe in polls.

J.F. This discussion is about Bob Packwood. And again I have to say the precedent set by the Senate Ethics Committee is for public hearings and that's the precedent that should be followed in the Packwood matter.

WPR. This is such a phony issue. Barbara Boxer has been ranting hysterically every night on television and is ready to tar and feather Bob Packwood. It's hyper ventilating feminists trying to muster support against Bob Packwood.

J.F. Those statements are so inappropriate, I don't care to comment. Before we get to the end of the program I want you to know I feel like I'm talking to neighbors. I'm a graduate of the University of Minnesota. When I was in school, I spent a couple of great football weekends in Madison—well, one of them wasn't so great. I watched

POWER IN THE PEOPLE

Alan Amache tromp the Golden Gophers. (I don't know what affect it had on the audience, but it gave me a chance to defuse my anger.)

WPR. We're about out of time.

J.F. Thanks so much, Tom. It's nice to talk with you.

Go back over my answers. How did I "touch and go?" How did I REPEAT, REPEAT, REPEAT the three main messages?

Over the years I've learned that, with some practice, everyone can respond well to questions. To get some experience, draft ten tough questions and write answers you'd use during the Q & A following a speech or in an interview. Then tape record those answers five times. Listen to how much more confident you sound after the fifth time.

PART III

GETTING ACTION
Turning Goals into Reality

Now that you know how to create a politically positive environment, let's turn your goals into reality by turning the heat up and keeping pressure on until—and even after—you've got the action you want by lobbying, testifying, monitoring, working inside the system, supporting and electing public officials, working with officials' staff members, and using the legal system if you have to.

12

LOBBYING

The Golden Rule of Politics:

**Do unto others as you would have them do unto you . . .
ESPECIALLY POLITICIANS AND THEIR STAFF MEMBERS!**

What is effective grassroots lobbying?

It's Alice Paul sending ten-women brigades to stand by the White House gates every day during World War I so when President Woodrow Wilson leaves the grounds, he must pass their banners:

> MR. PRESIDENT, WHAT WILL YOU DO FOR WOMEN SUFFRAGE?
> HOW LONG MUST WOMEN WAIT FOR LIBERTY?

It's a League of Women Voters chapter in the mid-sixties taking a conservative southern Senator, adamantly opposed to federal programs, to meet families with little food in their shacks. These face-to-face meetings convert the Senator into a champion for federally funded food programs.

POWER IN THE PEOPLE

And it's a tiny group of determined Oregonians with limited funds forming the *National Coalition For Public Hearings in the Packwood Matter* proving there really *is* power IN the people!

When Senate offices opened on Monday, November 1, 1993, each had a three-page faxed letter waiting to be read. The signers of the letter, a broad-based list of seventy-two leaders of civic, religious, and women's organizations from across the nation, grabbed readers' attention. The list included presidents of the National Association of Commissions for Women, BPW/USA (Business and Professional Women), National Association of Female Executives, National Women's Political Caucus, Fund for the Feminist Majority and National Organization for Women (NOW); religious leaders from Church Women United, United Church of Christ, and the Episcopal Church; lawyers, authors and famous women. It included leaders from Ethics Committee members' home states and Oregon.

"Inside the beltway" politicos said we couldn't win. But those voices didn't know about our broad-based coalition, the letter, or the strategy to be sure the letter with its impressive list of signers got attention in hectic Senate offices at the crucial moment. Shortly before the vote by the full Senate the next day, interns from NOW delivered the personally addressed original of the letter to each Senator's office. This boldly printed notice on bright red paper was stapled on the front:

**In an unprecedented, coordinated effort,
72 leaders of women's, civic and religious organizations
from across the nation join together to
congratulate the Ethics Committee on its work
in the Packwood matter, and call for setting a date
for public hearings to begin on the
completed parts of its investigation
without waiting to determine if
there are more areas to investigate.**

LOBBYING

The vote: **ninety-four to six to allow the Ethics Committee to subpoena Packwood's diaries!**

There's power in numbers, too. In November 1995, the United States House of Representatives considered a bill that would have stopped the Environmental Protection Agency (EPA) from enforcing seventeen current laws and rules. Those laws and rules included protecting wetlands, restricting the amount of arsenic in drinking water, and limiting air pollution by industry. On the day of the vote, environmental groups presented leaders of the House with the "Environmental Bill of Rights." After two close votes (212-206 and a 210-210 tie) against the EPA earlier in the year, this third attempt failed "handily" with a 227-194 vote. The power of 1.2 million signatures on a petition made a difference. And it made a BIG difference because they were delivered at the crucial time!

Effective lobbying is citizens individually or collectively through organizations communicating and advocating about concerns that can be handled by government. One of the Legislators of the Year honored by the alumni association of my alma mater, the University of Minnesota, Representative Becky Kelso commented, "I think it's safe to say that for any legislator, a letter or phone call or visit from the folks at home has far more clout than any paid lobbyist. People underestimate their own ability to influence legislators."

Legislators weigh conflicting interests communicated to them by individual citizens, organizations representing numbers of members and paid lobbyists—then they set public policy. We must always remember: Lobbying is an important part of the democratic process.

Town/Big City and Local/State/Federal

The size of legislative bodies and the number of constituents varies tremendously. The policy-setting entity of many municipal governments has five or seven members; the Council

POWER IN THE PEOPLE

of the City of Los Angeles has fifteen. Many legislators in small communities are part-time volunteers; Los Angeles City Council members are full-time, paid annual salaries of $98,069.97, and have up to fifteen full-time staff members. They each represent about 300,000 residents; that's about three-fourths the population of the state of Wyoming! The Oregon legislature meets every other year for about six months, unless there's a special session; the California legislature meets all year, every year.

The number of members of Congress each state has indicates the size of a state's population. California, the most populated state in the nation, has fifty-two representatives in Congress, New York has thirty-one, and Texas has thirty. The states of Alaska, Delaware, Montana, North Dakota, South Dakota, Vermont and Wyoming each have one member in the House of Representatives.

The number of members in the legislative body you're trying to influence, the number of constituents they represent, and the number of staff members they have are factors that affect the decision-making process and, therefore, determine how to effectively lobby. The smaller the constituency, the more direct contact between constituents and their legislators. The larger the constituency, the less direct contact between citizens and their legislators—and the more important role the staff plays. In Congress, in fact, staff members affect the content of legislation; often they even write it. The Congress has a much more complex structure than smaller local governments. Committee and subcommittee staff members are very important!

So you have an understanding of the task, find out:

1. How many people each legislator represents;
2. How much their salaries are;
3. If they have staff members and if they do, how many.

LOBBYING

LOBBYING AFTER TERM LIMITS

The passage of term limits in a number of states has changed the old rules of lobbying. No one is sure how. Two changes we do know for sure:

1. The role of staff members will be more important than ever.
2. The seniority system won't be used in the selection of committee and subcommittee chairs.

BEFORE YOU LOBBY

Here are the rules for an effective citizen lobbyist:

1. *Always tell the truth.* Good relationships are built on trust.
2. *Know your facts.* You've already done this. (Review the work you did in Chapter Five.)
3. *Know how the system works.* If you want to get a law passed you need to know how to get one written and introduced, how it works through the legislative process, and how it gets amended.
4. *Identify key legislators.* Find out how to get sponsors, who the key legislators on the issue are, and who should ask them for their support.
5. *Know the legislators you need to persuade.* Build a file of their voting record on similar issues, who influences their decisions, who their major contributors are, their special interests and occupation before being elected, other legislative experience, family background. You're not playing FBI; you're looking for clues on how to get them to work with you.
6. *Know their staff members.* These important people help you get work done inside the legislator's office. They often draft legislation and advise legislators on issues. If they believe in your cause, they may help you.

POWER IN THE PEOPLE

7. *Know other people in the process.* Know department heads because they advise legislators. Know members of sub-committees so your thoughts are included in their considerations as they work on legislation with other legislators' staff members.
8. *Know and obey all laws and regulations regarding lobbying.* Don't put the legislator, their staff members or your Action Committee in an awkward situation or a potentially damaging position. (Check back to Chapter Four.)
9. *Prepare materials for your members.* They'll need to have key points; a bill number; names, addresses, phone and fax numbers for the legislators they need to contact; they need to be told when to communicate.

U.S. Senators	General Senate Switchboard 202/225-3121
State Senators	Call Information

    The Honorable (name of senator)
    United States Senate
    Washington, DC 20510

    Dear Senator (name of senator):

Members of Congress	General House Switchboard 202/225-3121
State Houses and	
Local Legislators	Call Information

    The Honorable (name of member)
    United States House of Representatives
    Washington, DC 20515-1101

    Dear (Mr., Mrs., Ms. name):

Get the names, addresses, phone, fax and e-mail numbers of the legislators you need to work with to get your law passed.

LOBBYING

MEETING WITH LEGISLATORS

Remember, legislators and their staff members are very busy people. Few of us could or would be willing to deal with the numbers of issues we expect them to be experts on at the same time they deal with hundreds/thousands/millions of constituents.

Here are some guidelines to make your lobbying experience positive:

1. *Meet legislators in their districts, if possible.* Too often when they're in session, they're reviewing pending legislation, caucusing, attending subcommittee and committee meetings, working with staff members, or going to the floor to vote. They may be busy when they're home, but I've found them more likely to pay attention to me when we meet in their district offices.

2. *Take a team of three supporters.* As we do when meeting editorial boards, take people representing different organizations within the Action Committee. Be sure the legislator knows which of you are constituents, campaign volunteers, and contributors. One of you is the facilitator, making introductions and keeping things running smoothly. Each person talks about the issue from a different point of view; of course, all of you answer questions.

NEVER UNDER ANY CIRCUMSTANCES GO ALONE! Be sure:

- All points are covered;
- There are no misunderstandings about what is agreed to;
- There's a double check of your perceptions of the dynamics of the situation.

3. *Make good use of the limited time you'll have with the legislator.* Never expect a meeting to last more than ten or fifteen minutes. Each of your team members should have a

POWER IN THE PEOPLE

three-minute presentation covering such topics as: What the issue is. Why it's important. How much it will cost. Where the funds might be found in the budget. Who supports it. How large the coalition is.

STANDARD LOBBYING TACTICS

When people think of lobbying, they think of phoning or writing.

1. *Swamp them with phone calls.* Legislators are interested in hearing from informed, concerned constituents.
2. *Bury them with mail.* Encourage supporters to write—even a postcard. Legislators who expect to be reelected are responsive to their constituents. BEWARE: Letters that look mass produced, rather than original, are ignored!
3. *Send them a fax.* It's a quick, easy way to send a message.
4. *Or e-mail.* It's even quicker and easier.

When writing a member of Congress or state legislator, send an original letter to the district office and an original of the same letter to the office in the capitol. You may not know whether the key staff person is in the capitol or district office that week, or where the tally on issues is being kept. By sending to both offices, you've covered your bases.

CREATIVE GRASSROOTS LOBBYING TACTICS

**Lobbying should be more than
meeting legislators in their offices.
Anyone can do that.
Be creative. Be effective.
Prove there's a need.
Show that your cause has strong grassroots support.
Make legislators true believers, too!**

LOBBYING

In addition to meeting, letter writing, and phoning, here are some creative lobbying tactics to consider:

1. *Show decision-makers your polls.* They need to know your cause is popular.
2. *Present legislators with petitions.* Like Alice Paul, present them in a dramatic way.
3. *Lobby with visuals.* Remember the Florida Chamber of Commerce's success in defeating the proposal of their state's Department of Labor? The Chamber copied faxes from members on bright, red paper to make a graphic display of "red tape." As a result of this very visual third-of-a-mile of "red tape," the Department of Labor withdrew its proposal.

    Other visuals that help people understand your issue include videos, charts, pictures, and maps.
4. *Go-see trips.* Like the League of Women Voters learned, taking a legislator to see a tragic, human condition first hand can have a powerful impact. Go-see trips are great for environmental and land use issues, too.
5. *Place an ad.* On the next page is an ad that got lots of attention. We placed it in *The Washington Post*; other national media included it in news reports. The ad let Senators know we were playing "hardball." Media consultant Mandy Grunwald gets credit for the creativity and the design. We get credit for being "eggsy" and borrowing several thousand dollars to pay for it. We knew we were getting close to the end and believed we had to turn up the heat.

POWER IN THE PEOPLE

If your boss stuck his tongue in your mouth, would he keep his job? Only in the U.S. Senate.

17 women have accused Senator Bob Packwood of sexual misconduct. Everything from pushing staff members onto couches and pinning them down while he kissed them, to repeatedly grabbing women and forcing his tongue into their mouths.

And he's been accused of tampering with evidence and using his office in five separate attempts to solicit jobs for his ex-wife to avoid paying alimony.

The Senate Ethics Committee has found substantial credibility in all these charges.

What's happened to Senator Packwood in the two and a half years since these charges were made? <u>He's been promoted.</u>

After all the accusations were made public, Packwood was made chairman of the most powerful committee in the U.S. Senate.

Now, Majority Leader Bob Dole and the rest of the Senate must decide whether to hold public hearings or keep this matter behind closed doors.

Never before has the Ethics Committee concluded its process <u>without</u> public hearings.

The women have a right to be heard. Americans have a right to the truth.

LOBBYING

6. *Hold a rally.* This gets you media coverage—especially useful if you're in a situation where the "messengers are more important than the message." *The Willamette Week* sponsored a GROUND BOB DAY with the theme: Come out and see the light of day, Bob. It got great coverage, put some humor in a serious issue, and gave people something to rally around. Copies of the coverage were sent to Senators in D.C. so they didn't think we were just sitting around in the bleak midwinter waiting for them to do something.

FOLLOW UP

Always send a thank you note ASAP after a meeting. Thank the legislator and any staff members who were present for their advice, input, support—whatever is appropriate. The letter is as an opportunity to REPEAT your main messages. Use the letter, too, to restate your understanding of any agreements reached during the meeting.

If you haven't gotten a reply to a letter or phone call in two weeks, make another contact "just to touch base." Remember, your issue isn't legislators' top priority yet. You've got to keep it in front of them.

**Assume your lobbying effort is going to be successful!
But just in case it isn't,
remember the decision isn't about you personally.**

**Follow the Golden Rule.
You never know when you'll need to work with these legislators and their staff members again.**

13

TESTIFYING AT PUBLIC HEARINGS

My Dad:

They put their pants on like everyone else!

Back in the days when I was a "timid soul," I had a recurring nightmare. I would walk down the center aisle of the Orange County, California Board of Supervisors hearing room, up to a marble wall eight-feet tall, and look up to see five, white-haired, stern-faced, bespectacled men glowering down on me.

While hearing rooms with officials glowering down on citizens may be appropriate in dictatorships or monarchies, they're not appropriate for our democracy. So when I was asked to talk with the architect about my views and visions for the to-be-constructed Huntington Beach City Hall, I agreed. Result: That City Council Chamber was designed theater style, with Council members seated at a table on the floor and citizens looking down on them. I don't think anyone should be looking down on others, but this seating is a truer reflection of what democracy is about than are kings perched high on thrones.

POWER IN THE PEOPLE

Knowing how terrified I was of testifying gives me great admiration for ten-year-old Walter Dawson, a fifth-grader from Falls City, Oregon, who spoke to the United States Senate Committee on Aging in Washington, D.C. As part of the movement to get long-term care covered in a national health care package, he spoke *forcefully* about the devastating effect Alzheimer's disease had on his father and the financial hardship it brought to his family. When he was done, some wept, and others tightened their jaws and looked grimly ahead. Now, that's powerful testimony!

But to be effective in lobbying takes much more than powerful testimony. It takes hard work, strategic planning, preparation. Too often citizens waltz into a City Council meeting expecting to have their say and get their way. When they don't, they claim the system is "rigged."

Think about it. If you were an elected official going to vote on an important issue—a stop sign on a dangerous corner, a reading curriculum, long-term health care—would you wait until a public hearing to think about it? If you're the kind of elected official I want in public office you do your homework. For the stop sign, you've been to the site, talked with the police and transportation departments. For a reading curriculum, you've talked with reading specialists, school administrators, teachers, parents, students. For health care reform, you've listened to health care professionals and patients. Whatever the issue, by the time of the public hearing, you could very well be on the way to making a decision. Or even have made it. Responsible legislators make decisions based on facts, not just last minute emotional appeals.

So it may not be that the system is "rigged." It may be that some people—effective citizen groups and major corporations—know how to use it. They do all the things we've been talking about. Build effective coalitions. Poll so they know there is consensus in their community on the issue and have messages that

TESTIFYING . . .

move people to their point of view. Get editorial support. Write lots of letters to the editor. Speak at civic clubs. Lobby.

And they do things we haven't talked about. They work in candidate campaigns. And they contribute money to campaigns.

People who understand the democratic process know that testifying is just one step near the end of a long process. Like everything else we've talked about, you must prepare carefully to testify successfully.

1. *Select a captain and insist that everyone follow his or her direction.* A colleague and the organization he represents had done a great job of lobbying and had lined up the four votes from a seven-member committee they needed to kill a politically appealing, but bad, bill. On the day before the vote, their fourth vote announced he would leave the hearing at 11:30 the next morning to go to the races; If people wanted his vote, they needed to get it before then. At 11:15 on race day, he made the announcement again. My friend tried unsuccessfully to persuade a "team(?)" member not to testify. "I've driven here twice and I'm going to give my statement!" At 11:30—as the testifier droned on—the fourth vote left. All the hard work was down the drain! This was no nightmare. It's a true story.

2. *Handpick your testifiers.* You want people who support your issue for different reasons and will connect with the different political points of view on the legislative body. Ask yourself: Who among our supporters will have the most credibility with members of the board or council? Bring prestige? Expertise? Speak to the ethic diversity of the board or council?

3. *Prepare statements in advance.* For local governments—city councils and school boards—keep statements to one page. If you've done your lobbying work well, elected officials or board members already know the facts. This is

POWER IN THE PEOPLE

the time to simply remind them of the most important reasons for them to support your issue.

It has more impact and credibility to have twenty people giving twenty different points of view than one person giving them all. Each statement by a leader from an organization includes:

- the name of the presenter;
- her or his address and telephone number;
- a title. It can be as simple as, "Testimony in favor of _____";
- the date;
- the name of the organization;
- the number of members the organization has;
- the main reasons for the organization's position.

Statements of people speaking as individuals include:

- the same information as the first four points above;
- their relevant personal background, experience and expertise;
- the main reasons for their interest in the issue.

Put the most important information in the first paragraph. You'll see why in a minute. Say thank you at the end of your statement.

4. *Review all statements in advance.* Look at the statements as a package. Be sure all key points are covered and all parts of your coalition are represented.

5. *Make copies.* Have enough copies of all statements to give one to each member of the legislative body, staff members, department heads, and the media.

6. *Have speakers in assigned order.* Put them in an order that makes impact. If I had Walter Dawson, the ten-year-old who caused people to weep, in my group, I'd put him last.

7. *Pack the hearing room.* Especially on controversial issues, it's vital to have lots of people so legislators are confident that they're not out there all alone twisting in the wind.

TESTIFYING . . .

8. *Have supporters make a visual statement.* For the stop-sign issue, people might wear political buttons or children's pictures. For a reading curriculum issue, school T-shirts. For health care, doctors' white coats or just plain white shirts/blouses. Here's a time to be creative!

At the public hearing:

1. *Respect legislators' time and energy.* If you're like most Americans, you never attend public hearings or council meetings—but the people you're talking to sit through hundreds of hours of them. Give each of them copies of all the statements your group has prepared, but have testifiers read only their first paragraphs!

   If other people have made your points, don't repeat them. Simply say that you agree with points that have been made.

   This issue may be your top priority. Legislators have to deal with the top priorities of dozens of constituents.

2. *If you have a great visual—a chart, an enlargement of a dramatic photograph, a blue print or model—put it up for the entire hearing on your issue.* That will reenforce your message and give the media a good "photo op."

3. *Say thank you.* "For your time." "For your consideration." ASAP after the hearing, say thank you again in a brief note. Everyone needs strokes! Be a graceful winner or loser.

Now:

1. Make a timeline so you know when you need statements to allow enough time to review them as a package;
2. Make a list of the people you want to testify;

POWER IN THE PEOPLE

3. Recruit them. Explain to each one the importance of working as a team. Suggest the key point for him or her to include.
4. Tell people by what date you'd like to have their statements.

To be more democratic, you may wish to review the statements with the whole group together. Once you know all the key points are covered, be sure enough copies are made.

If you won, congratulations!
If you didn't, go back and think ...
what you might have done differently or better.
Losing is not always someone else's fault.

14

OBSERVING AND MONITORING

If you take a woman fishing, she has to be a dull one. Anyone lively scares away the fish.

Elizabeth Jenkins

Here's a BIG-fish-that-got-away story! One League of Women Voters' observer of the Orange County, California Board of Supervisors noticed that the 1994 county budget balanced its general fund with 3 percent of its revenue from interest on investments; the 1995 budget showed 35 percent from interest on investments! She had just started asking questions about how investment revenues could skyrocket ten times in one year when the tidal wave hit. Some people claim "poor management," "misconduct," and senior brokerage executives "wantonly and callously selling risky investments" led to the $1.7 billion financial crash that ultimately forced the Orange County government into bankruptcy.

The crash could have been avoided if only someone had been observing or monitoring the government more closely. No one was. Not elected officials. Not the brokerage house. Not the media. Not citizens. No one was watching.

POWER IN THE PEOPLE

No one on the inside who was aware of the "risky investments" was courageous enough to stand up publicly against greed.

The moral of this story: Americans must watch their government!

Let's talk for a few minutes about two different roles—observers and monitors—to do the watching.

1. Observers are passive watchers of public decision-making bodies. They witness the conduct and competence of their officials.
2. Monitors are the public "whistle-blowers" who know how the decision-making process is supposed to work and also know what actions on specific issues their organizations support.

The observer corps is one of my first memories of the League of Women Voters. We were the "eyes and ears" of the public at city council, school board, county, and state government meetings. It's one of the things new members were encouraged to do so they learned how government works and about the abilities and personalities of elected officials. What a service they provided!

These watchdogs for the public sat through hours upon hours of meetings, as do legislators. You've noticed, I suppose, that this is written in the past tense.

I've just phoned several Leagues in different parts of the nation looking for observer corps success stories to share with you. Unfortunately, this valuable community service program is apparently the victim of a lack of volunteers.

That's too bad because there are many benefits of an observer corps. They:

1. "Identify issues and trends" in the community and report their observations back to their organizations for action;
2. Alert the media to an area of special community concern;

OBSERVING AND MONITORING

3. Increase the visibility and enhance the image of their organization among elected and appointed officials and among community leaders and citizens concerned about good government;
4. Learn what lobbying techniques are effective with each policy-making body;
5. Learn what officials are "approachable" and what points to make and avoid with them in areas of special concern to their organizations;
6. Learn to pick the right time to lobby; and,
7. It's a terrific stepping stone to elected and appointed offices.

Louise Questad, of the League of Women Voters of Portland, Oregon, used to be a loyal League observer. Like me, she thinks it's a very valuable community service. But she points out that the observer program in Portland has evolved into an even more beneficial service. She recalls that some twenty years ago elected officials and government department heads were irritated with "citizens sticking their noses in the government's business." Things have changed. Government—at least here in Portland—has become a much more open process with many avenues for citizen participation on advisory committees.

One recent success regards the Regional Water Supply Committee recommendation that our city's drinking water come from the Willamette River. The citizens' advisory committee, which studied the issue for several years, recommended other options. It's the citizens' advisory committee's proposal that is being forwarded to the Council for action.

But without the League's observer corps, individuals are filling the void. Citizen-activist, Ralph Bauer, in Huntington Beach, California, for example, served as a one-person observer corps for his community. He attended city council meetings for more than a year, found citizens dissatisfied about a number

POWER IN THE PEOPLE

of neighborhood issues, compiled a list of people and organizations who testified, used the list to build a city-wide coalition, and ultimately won a seat on the city council. Thank goodness, for people like Ralph.

If you want to fill this void in your community, it's good manners and common courtesy to send a letter of introduction to the chair of the body. Here's a sample for you to adapt to your own needs.

(insert date)

(insert name)
(insert title)
(insert name of government body)
(insert address)
(insert city, state, zip)

Dear *(insert name):*

During the next several months, (name of observer) of the (name of your group) will be an observer at the meetings of (the government body).

(Observer's name) will listen but not participate in your group's meetings. In this way, our organization will be informed on the community issues that are of special interest to us.

Any assistance you can give, such as providing advance copies of agendas and materials for public distribution, notices of special meetings and public hearings, will be very helpful and greatly appreciated.

Please send them to: *(Observer's name)*
                       (Observer's address)
                       (Observer's city, state, zip)
                       Phone number: *(observer's number)*
                       Fax number: *(observer's number)*

If you have any questions or comments, please call me at (your telephone number). Thank you.

Sincerely,

(your name)
(your title)

OBSERVING AND MONITORING

Such a letter or a telephone call would have saved one school board some anxiety. I don't remember why four of us women decided to attend the board meeting one night some twenty years ago. I do remember that five male board members became very quiet and exchanged worried looks when we entered the room. In those days there were lots of "special interest" groups dropping into school board meetings in Orange County.

Thanks to the League of Women Voters of the Greater Dayton, Ohio Area for letting me share their General Guidelines for Observers from the *Observer's Manual*.

- Be a good listener; that is, be able to concentrate on, assimilate, and interpret proceedings with objective summaries of controversial issues.
- Become familiar with the organization, functions and operations of the agency observed and thus able to relate the formal decisions with the day-to-day performance.
- Be interested in local government processes, policy formulation, and responsiveness to citizen concerns.
- Identify problems, proposals, and actions that bear upon League program items or that might be significant in future program development.
- Exercise discretion and tact at meetings; keep in mind pressures and demands made on elected officials.
- Be courteous and appreciative of help offered.
- Attend meetings regularly, arrive on time, and stay through the entire meeting.

I would add only one item to the list. Observers should wear an organization button or name tag—something to identify them to the board, council, or commission members. It would also be a reminder that their constituents are watching.

POWER IN THE PEOPLE

When keeping a record of the policy-making bodies' activities and action, it is important for the observer to make a written report that includes:

1. *Date of the meeting*
2. *Name of the council, board, or commission observed*
3. *Names of voting members present*
4. *Names of voting members absent*
5. *Names of managers and department heads present*
6. *Names of managers and department heads absent*
7. *Media present*
8. *Organizations and special interest groups present*
9. *Actions taken on issues of concern to your group*
    Management recommendations on each issue:
    - Persons, organizations and special interest groups speaking for the issue
    - Persons, organizations and special interest groups speaking against it
    - Members voting for it
    - Members voting against it
    - Special comments and recommendations
10. *Actions postponed and reasons for postponements*:
    - Management recommendations on each issue
    - Persons, organizations and special interest groups speaking for postponement
    - Persons, organizations and special interest groups speaking against postponement
    - Members voting for postponement
    - Members voting against postponement
    - Reasons given for postponement
    - Date the issue is to be on the agenda again
    - Special comments and recommendations
11. *Future dates for items of interest to your group:*

OBSERVING AND MONITORING

Here's a sample observer's form for you to adapt to your needs:

OBSERVER'S REPORT

Observer _____ Meeting of _____
Date _____ Starting time _____ Ending time _____
Members present _____
Members absent _____
Staff present _____
Media present _____
Others of note present _____

Agenda Items   *Actions Taken*
_____   _____
_____   _____
_____   _____
_____   _____
_____   _____

Items Postponed   *Reasons for Postponements*
_____   _____
_____   _____
_____   _____
_____   _____
_____   _____

Dates to note _____

Comments/Recommendations
_____
_____
_____
_____
_____
_____
_____
_____
_____

POWER IN THE PEOPLE

HOLD THE PEOPLE YOU ELECT ACCOUNTABLE

Someone from your organization has sat through hours and hours of public hearings, kept good notes and filed them. What for? People who have served as observers will tell you that their mere presence made a difference in how members of the board acted and how they conducted the public's business. That alone is a victory for people power.

But there's much more you can do with the information observers have collected:

1. *Report the information to organizations on the Action Committee* and they in turn can report to their memberships in newsletters, bulletins, ACTION ALERTS.

2. *Publicize voting records.* Place an ad in your local newspaper listing incumbents' voting records on key issues.

3. *Make an election issue of their attendance.* If an incumbent you're working to defeat has missed a number of key votes, be sure it becomes an election issue. At candidate forums, speaking opportunities, and news conferences ask why the incumbent was absent when key votes were taken.

4. *Use the information in fund-raising.* Think about this for a teaser on a fund-raising letter and the first line of a letter: How many bad checks did your Congressman write?

5. *Alert the media* to positive and negative information about members' decision- making, voting records, inconsistencies between campaign promises and actions taken.

6. *Inform community opinion leaders* about a legislator's votes.

15

WORKING ON THE INSIDE

About my great grandfather, George W. Confer:

His life so pure and tender and lofty shall be an inspiration to better and truer aims in life, and influence us toward a higher and nobler sense of civic duty.

The Minneapolis Chronicle
January 23, 1904

"Keith mentored me on the notion of creating a position for community colleges within the U.S. Department of Education. We worked in partnership, under his vision, to conquer the Washington bureaucracy. It took us five years and great patience from the time Keith brought the idea forward to enact legislation, fund the position and see an Oregonian—Betty Duvall—appointed as the first federal liaison for community colleges." So wrote Senator Mark Hatfield in a letter read by his wife at Keith Skelton's memorial service.

Former Congressman Les AuCoin, who lost the very close 1992 election for the United States Senate from Oregon to Bob Packwood, spoke at the service about his work with Keith on this

POWER IN THE PEOPLE

same issue in the United States House of Representatives.

Until this success, there hadn't been one staff member within the Department with a degree from a community college or who came from a community college setting. That meant no one with personal experience of the value of community colleges was "inside" as an advocate. Now there is.

What a perfect example of working on the inside! And of lobbying, tenacity, and working both sides of the aisle—Mark Hatfield is Republican; Keith Skelton and Les AuCoin, Democrats.

Having allies in decision-making positions—the local planning commission, the state fish and wildlife commission, or a federal department—makes an action committee's success more likely. You get your point of view included in setting legislative priorities, drafting legislation, and in preliminary budget discussions. It's harder to get input after the machine has started moving. Sometimes it seems like standing in front of a steamroller. Other times like trying to break up cement with a toothpick!

Now find answers to these questions:

1. *What committees or commissions in the government have authority on your issue?* Parents' committee on school issues? Planning commission on land use? Citizens' committee on health care?
2. *How does someone get to serve on the government body that acts on your issue?* Appointment? Election? Just show up and volunteer?
3. *What are the requirements and responsibilities?* How often are meetings held? How long do they last? When? Where? Are members paid? If travel is required, is there a travel allowance?
4. *How many people are in the group?* If it's a seven-member planning commission, for example, you may want to work over a period of time to get four people on the commission so your point of view controls the decisions.

WORKING ON THE INSIDE

With the answers in hand, recruit someone from your Committee to join or apply for. Look for someone who is strong, but polite; committed to the cause, but can negotiate; knows the facts, but "doesn't know it all." You're looking, too, for someone who understands how the legislative process works, can work both sides of the aisle, and who has the ability, commitment, and time to do the job very well. A competent person inside helps win other insiders, elected officials, and the general public to your point of view.

Once you've recruited her or him, you may have to spend more time, effort, and perhaps a little money. The Action Committee may have to lobby to get the person you want in the position you need him or her in. And don't forget: You'll have to be there with hand holding and hand clapping when things get tough.

The kind words for my great grandfather might have been written for Keith Skelton.

16

SUPPORTING SUPPORTIVE PUBLIC OFFICIALS

Thank you for your generous comments about my role in the Packwood case, which I read in the National Journal . . . I won't forget them.

Senator Mitch McConnell,
Chairman of the Senate Ethics Committee

And those of us who worked on behalf of Bob Packwood's accusers won't forget the courage, integrity, and leadership of Republican Senator McConnell from Kentucky, Chairman of the Ethics Committee, during the last year of the "Packwood matter," and of Democrat Senator Richard Bryan of Nevada, Chairman of the Committee, during the beginning years of the long ordeal.

Bouquets of red roses to each of them and their Senate Ethics Committee colleagues: Republicans Larry E. Craig, Idaho; Robert C. Smith, New Hampshire; and Democrats Barbara A. Mikulski, Maryland; Thomas A. Daschle, who was on the Committee until he became Senate Minority Leader in 1995, South Dakota; and Byron L. Dorgan, North Dakota, who replaced

POWER IN THE PEOPLE

Senator Daschle. They and the Committee staff all served the Senate and the nation with great distinction.

"Thank you" and "congratulations" are such easy words to say or write to elected officials who have done the right thing. They are words that need to be said more often to elected and appointed officials and to others who make a difference in our lives.

Here are some ways to say those "three little words" publicly:

1. *In media interviews.* After a major news event, the media calls their contacts for comments on an issue. That's how I happened to be quoted in the *National Journal.* Their reporter called to interview me after the Ethics Committee voted six to zero to recommend to the full Senate that Packwood be expelled.

2. *In news conferences.* After the Arkansas Supreme Court removed Amendment 6 from the ballot before the 1994 election, we called a news conference to declare victory—polls showed us on track to win by a three-to-one margin. We went on to thank "over 10,000 men and women and representatives of more than fifty of the state's most respected organizations who worked to defeat Amendment 6." This was the largest grassroots campaign committee on a ballot measure in Arkansas history.

3. *Publicize their voting records.* Use this information in your organization's newsletter to support the legislators who have voted the way you wanted them to.

4. *In print ads.* BLESS YOU, AMERICA. From The People Of Oklahoma. At the bottom of the ad, "The people of Oklahoma want to thank *Newsweek* for their extraordinary generosity in providing this space at no cost." In the awful Oklahoma City tragedy, the "vast, shining, outpouring, unprecedented in its depth, and scope, and need" proved what a compassionate people we are.

SUPPORTING . . . PUBLIC OFFICIALS

5. *At your meetings.* Honor supportive elected and appointed officials who have been especially supportive of your cause. Seat them at the head table of your annual dinner, acknowledge them with a plaque or award of the year, or at a general membership meeting.

   The Alumni Association of my alma mater, the University of Minnesota, honored four Minnesota legislators at the alumni association's 1995 Leadership Conference. The four who "really went to bat for the "U" were named Legislators of the Year by the association.

6. *At their town halls.* Many legislators hold town halls in their districts to listen to constituents' concerns. Since lots of people will be there to complain, it's an especially good time and place for you to say "thank you for your good work!"

7. *Use a skywriter.* When I asked Paige Richardson, district director for my United States Representative, what creative things people had done to thank Elizabeth Furse, she couldn't think of any. Then she paused and said, "But I've always thought it would be fun to write her name in the sky."

Here are other ways to say "thank you" and "congratulations" to elected and appointed officials and their staff members:

1. *Send a thank you note ASAP.* It isn't necessary to say a lot. "Thank you for your great support. We couldn't have won without you and your staff!" "Bouquets of yellow daffodils for your courageous vote! We're most grateful!" Many constituents write only to complain; most don't write at all.

2. *Call them.* That's easy, too. You already have their telephone numbers. They won't want to spend a long time on the phone. You can say something as simple as, "Senator

POWER IN THE PEOPLE

Jones, your leadership made the difference. On behalf of all 200 of our members, thank you and your staff members very much."

3. *Work for the officials' reelection.* Volunteer to walk precincts, stuff envelopes, phone to follow up on fund-raising letters or invitations to events, work on the get-out-the-vote effort. There are so many jobs you can pick from. Volunteer for just one.

4. *Contribute to their campaigns.* If you think it's a problem to have candidates accepting large contributions from a few "special interests," then be part of the solution by making small, regular contributions. Send your first check in the first week of the campaign—and then send a check every other month. Look at campaign contributions as investments in your community's future!

5. *Hold a fund-raising event.* Call the campaign office and volunteer to hold an event in your home or to sponsor a major fund-raising event with others. This is another way you can be part of the solution to the big-money, "special interest" groups having influence out of proportion to their number of votes.

6. *Help make the legislator a household name.* Tell people about his or her good works. Let people know this legislator listens to constituents, solves problems, shows leadership, is someone you trust and voters can count on—even though you don't agree on every issue.

7. *Stand up for your legislator.* If you hear someone making negative remarks about this supportive legislator, use Michael Sheehan's "touch and go" technique. Say, "I'm really surprised. My experience is that (and then "go" with your messages like those in the point above.)

8. *Be there in tough times.* When the official is facing a difficult, controversial vote—on your issue or other issues you

SUPPORTING . . . PUBLIC OFFICIALS

agree on—be there to support her or his courage. Help pack the hearing room. Have people wear something so it's obvious why you're there and who you're supporting.

Whatever you do to show support for supportive officials, be sure you follow your community's public disclosure and lobbying regulations. Some regulations forbid giving appointed or elected officials anything of value.

**Let supportive public officials know
you won't forget their good works!**

17

ELECTING SUPPORTIVE OFFICIALS

*Politics will be dirty business
as long as good people stay out of it!*

A Truism

There certainly is no better national example of electing supportive officials than the 1994 victory of Republicans gaining control of Congress. They set their agenda, selected districts polling showed they could take away from the Democrats, and recruited candidates in those districts they thought could win. Then they used strategic planning, effective media, money, time, and volunteers to be sure their candidates went to Washington, D.C. in January 1995.

If your Action Committee is failing to get the legislation passed you want because people in decision-making positions have a political philosophy that doesn't agree with your goals, then consider getting candidates who will work with you. You'll need to ask a lot of questions and be prepared to do a lot of work, but citizens in towns and cities across the nation have done it. You can, too!

POWER IN THE PEOPLE

Ask your Action Committee:

1. *Do we care enough about our community* to make electing supportive officials our only priority for action from now until election day?
2. *Are we committed to working together?*
3. *Do our organizations' agendas allow enough resources—* volunteers, money, talent—to successfully elect candidates?
4. *Do our organizations have the commitment needed to win?*
5. *Can we broaden our coalition to increase our chances of winning?* The people power successes in local candidate elections are often the result of people with common goals working together despite their partisan differences.
6. *What districts can we win?* Be sure your answer is realistic, rational and based the demographics of the district. Wishful thinking leads to disaster.

Now let's look at the personal traits of winning candidates.

1. They have led lives of integrity that are "squeaky clean" and can stand the close scrutiny of the opposition and the media. The "Packwood matter" and any number of election debacles are examples of the troubles you'll face if there are skeletons in the closet.
2. They want to win. Colin Powell's decision not to run for president because he didn't feel it in his blood was the right thing to do.
3. They have a supportive family and a large network of committed political allies and friends. Without this vital support, the candidate can easily become emotionally drained.
4. They and their families are willing to learn and take

ELECTING SUPPORTIVE OFFICIALS

advice. Lots of candidate campaign managers admit that the hardest part of their job is working with candidates' families.

5. They have self-confidence and the poise to handle high-pressure situations.
6. They have a competent, professional, and friendly manner.
7. They are physically and mentally strong.

>Now, let's look at the political qualities important to candidates winning.

1. They're well known in their communities.
2. They have a record of community involvement and activities.
3. There will be a number of credible endorsements for your candidate at the beginning of the campaign.
4. They know facts about their community and the campaign issues.
5. They can talk about these issues with ease.
6. They have a political philosophy that is consistent with the community they want to represent. My first campaign experience was in 1954 in the fall after I graduated from the University of Minnesota. A college friend, Dutch Cragen, and I worked for Ed Willow, Executive Director of the local YMCA and a candidate for Congress. It was a great learning experience even though Ed lost overwhelmingly. In hindsight, I shouldn't have been surprised. The northside district we were working for on behalf of a Republican candidate remains very Democratic to this day! The main lesson: If you want to win, work for a candidate whose political attitudes are generally consistent with the constituency she or he hopes to represent.
7. They can cite enough facts to give voters confidence.

POWER IN THE PEOPLE

If you and the Action Committee decide to recruit and support candidates, be sure to get them the very best advise available. Talk with people who have run for office—both those who won and those who didn't—to learn all the lessons you can. And, if you're considering backing a candidate for state or national office, seek counsel and support from your political party's state central committee and national committee. They have good candidate schools, reliable polling, and may even offer experienced staff and campaign funds.

18

USING THE LEGAL SYSTEM

Both politicians and journalists, (I add lawyers and political consultants) *must aim at serving the community which means morality in practice.*

Vaclav Havel,
President of the Czech Republic

Lawyers are as badly regarded as political consultants. Unfortunately, some rotten apples spoil the reputations of two fields filled with good people.

Many lawyers and law firms have a policy of doing "pro bono publico" work (Latin: for the public good; everyday language: free). Much of the work I've done with citizen grassroots efforts wouldn't have been possible or successful without the tremendous work of volunteer attorneys.

In the 1990 Oregon pro-choice campaign, for instance, Douglas C. Blomgren provided over $17,000 in free legal services! I called him so often, I still know his office phone number by memory. Doug guided me through campaign finance regula-

POWER IN THE PEOPLE

tions, political advertising requirements, contributions and expenditures reporting, and tax questions.

We had a couple of long Saturday morning conference calls with Eleanor Smeal, president of The Feminist Majority, and her attorneys working on a complaint to the Internal Revenue Service regarding activities of one of the largest foundations in the nation. Because all contributions to the Foundation are tax deductible, the Foundation is strictly prohibited from any political activity. Yet they ran $200,000 of radio spots about Measure 10! They spent lots more in two direct mail pieces—one a letter restating the message on the radio spots, the second a "be sure to vote" postcard delivered the weekend before the election. Because the Foundation did not report its spending, we don't know how much was spent. Because of the IRS's confidentiality policy, we never found out what happened as a result of our complaint.

In the "Packwood matter," more than two dozen attorneys provided free legal counsel for the various parts of the issue. One team of eight attorneys prepared a twenty-one-page petition on behalf of 250 Oregonians requesting that the United States Senate Rules Committee investigate claims that Packwood "was not duly elected" and "committed election fraud." Their petition was powerful! So powerful, in fact, that the Rules Committee held a public hearing—to the astonishment of cynical Washington "insiders."

None of us will ever forget watching the C-SPAN coverage. There was intelligent, forceful, lead counsel Katherine A. Meyer, with B. Carlton Grew at the counsel table, and Maureen Leonard as backup, making her statement and responding to tough questions by sixteen Senators in the Committee hearing room. Her voice was confident. Her answers clear, concise and to the point. The Committee ruled sixteen to zero against the petitioners but only on the grounds that the Ethics Committee, not the Rules Committee, was the appropriate forum to rule on Packwood's conduct.

USING THE LEGAL SYSTEM

A second team of fifteen attorneys represented all the courageous women who told the Ethics Committee staff about Packwood's acts of sexual misconduct against them. These attorneys helped the women file complaints with the Committee, prepared the women to give their depositions to the Committee staff, and advised them on a host of other issues.

More lawyers—both in Oregon and Washington, D.C.—assisted when their expertise was needed and their busy schedules allowed. Near the end of the long ordeal when it appeared there might be public hearings after all, the leaders of the National Women's Law Center and Women's Legal Defense League in Washington, D.C., called to say both organizations would provide pro bono legal services to the seventeen women whose charges of Packwood's sexual misconduct had been included in the list of "substantial credible evidence" cited in the Ethics Committee's resolution.

How do you find such qualified legal counsel?

Unfortunately, there isn't any one number to call. According to Ann Bartsch, Associate Executive Director, Oregon State Bar, you'll have to do some searching. She recommends you start by calling the bar association's referral service in your state. That service has a list of attorneys in good standing who want to do volunteer work for causes they believe in.

In addition to those lawyers, there are legal aid programs, consumer groups and government agencies that may help you. The Lawyers' Guild, American Civil Liberties Union (ACLU), and the state chapter of the American Trial Lawyers' Association are other possibilities. And, of course, when all else fails let your fingers go walking through the Yellow Pages.

Here are guidelines to remember when grassroots, citizens' groups file a lawsuit:

1. *There is strength in numbers*. "It is easier to intimidate one or two people than to squash a large active membership,"

POWER IN THE PEOPLE

according to Michael Williams, organizing director for the grassroots Citizen's Clearinghouse for Hazardous Waste.

2. *Build public awareness for your issue.* You've already done it in spades. But you've got to keep it up. It tells your opposition that your group is very serious!
3. *Be sure your statements are factually correct and legally sound.* You and your lawyer must be *very* sure!

No fear or risk is great enough to give up your right to speak out in every lawful way you can!

PART IV

THE BALLOT MEASURE
When All Else Fails

Bumper sticker:
> When the people lead,
> the leaders will follow.

STATES WITH A BALLOT MEASURE PROCESS

Alaska	Missouri
Arizona	Montana
Arkansas	Nebraska
California	Nevada
Colorado	North Dakota
Florida	Ohio
Idaho	Oklahoma
Illinois	Oregon
Maine	South Dakota
Massachusetts	Utah
Michigan	Washington state
Mississippi	Wyoming

POWER IN THE PEOPLE

Before we talk about how to win ballot measure campaigns, let's agree that—because there are as many variations on initiatives and referendums as Chopin wrote etudes—we'll call them all ballot measures. You'll want to ask your City Clerk's or Secretary of State's Offices what variations play in your state.

And another thing I want you to know before we talk about winning ballot measure campaigns is of my grave concerns about the abuses of them. Since the bulk of my work is managing ballot measure campaigns I'm keenly aware of the abuses and their consequences. I'm Senior Consultant with one of the premier ballot measure campaign management firms in the nation, Goddard*Claussen/First Tuesday. This firm of top-flight professionals has won 90 percent of its ballot measure campaigns. Working with three of my favorite men, Rick Claussen and Frank Schubert, both brilliant political strategists, and creative, Emmy-award-winning, Ben Goddard, is the greatest professional experience of my career. We all support the ballot measure process in principle; but my colleagues share my concerns about its abuses.

Supporters describe the ballot measure process as democracy in its purest form. I believe it's too often a repudiation of representative democracy. It allows elected officials to avoid making tough decisions on controversial issues. The process, designed with good intentions, is being used by special-interest groups to promote single-issue agendas and to offer "quick-fix" solutions to complex problems. These solutions circumvent the normal legislative process which, with all its imperfections, is far more likely to produce just, constitutional, reasonable, and workable laws than is the ballot measure process. Through the tedious, cumbersome legislative process there is compromise and balance, incorporating minority concerns with majority rights.

The ballot measure process is an odd phenomenon. Depending on the number of voters in a local ballot measure election, hundreds to thousands of voters decide on such diverse issues as school bonds, election procedures, government process.

THE BALLOT MEASURE

In a statewide ballot measure election, hundreds of thousands to millions of voters walk into election booths and individually express their opinions. Together these voters make laws on subjects as diverse as tax structures, the criminal justice system, civil rights, and environmental protection.

Too often, voters know little about the complex issues they decide in ballot measure elections. Their decisions may be based only on a ten-word summary of the measure. They seldom see, much less read, the long, complex proposed law with all its fine print. The more in-depth basis for their decisions are thirty- and sixty-second television spots and news coverage that lasts an average of twenty seconds.

They don't understand the consequences and costs, sometimes hidden, of the measure. They forget about the millions of consumer and shareholder dollars spent on the most controversial ballot measure campaigns. And they forget the millions of taxpayer dollars spent on years of legal challenges moving through an already over-burdened court system all the way to the United States Supreme Court.

It's difficult to undo bad ballot measures that require another vote in many states or super majorities in state legislatures!

The ballot measure process is a permanent part of participatory democracy in twenty-four states, about four-fifths of them west of the Mississippi River, and the District of Columbia. The process is used more and more frequently. In 1970, there were ten statewide ballot measures in the nation. On the November 1994 ballot in my state of Oregon there were eighteen ballot measures ranging from tax issues to campaign finance, from assisted suicide to child pornography, and from gay rights to public employee pension benefits. Two of the measures were referred to voters by the State Senate, the other sixteen by groups of citizens each collecting nearly 100,000 signatures!

POWER IN THE PEOPLE

Americans in all regions of the nation overwhelmingly support the ballot measure process. So it's here to stay. Let's look at how to win.

19

THE BALLOT MEASURE

*Different issues, different circumstances,
different people, different times
get different results.*

There's no perfect formula for a successful ballot measure campaign. Each situation is unique, requiring a comprehensive campaign strategy based upon in-depth public opinion polling results—we talked about those earlier.

CANDIDATE AND BALLOT MEASURE CAMPAIGNS ARE VARIED

Because candidate campaigns are so different from ballot measure campaigns, it's impossible to transfer skills from one to the other.

While it's less true than a decade ago, candidate campaigns still are more stable than ballot measure campaigns because of political party allegiances, partisan ideology, and regional and ethnic alliances. Volunteers are attracted to candidate campaigns because they believe in and like to be close to a

POWER IN THE PEOPLE

candidate. Fund-raising is easier because contributors will have a responsive person or political leverage if their candidate wins. Why else do corporations and lobbyists often contribute to both candidates for the same office?

On the other hand, ballot measure campaigns have no "personality," and often no tangible benefits after the election except a new law or a law not enacted. Ballot measure campaigns have only ideas to sell. In ballot measure campaigns, messages are easier to control because spokespersons are carefully selected and trained. Fund-raising and volunteer recruitment are much harder than in candidate campaigns.

To win requires that you define the debate. And that you define it early in your terms! In the 1990 Oregon pro-choice campaign, we didn't talk about abortion, we said, "No going back to back-alley abortions." In the 1994 Arkansas campaign we didn't talk about "AN AMENDMENT TO THE ARKANSAS CONSTITUTION TO RESTRUCTURE THE WORKERS' COMPENSATION COMMISSION AND REVISE WORKERS' COMPENSATION LAW." We said, "AMENDMENT 6, IT'S A JOB KILLER!" In 1992, Goddard*Claussen/First Tuesday, in another of its nationally recognized ballot measure campaigns, didn't debate the need for health care reform, just that "single payer" wasn't the solution to the problem of increasing medical costs and decreasing health care quality.

Messages must be clear, concise, credible, consistent, and factual. Debating the other sides' issues detracts from your messages and isn't an effective use of resources. Winning campaigns use their time by REPEATING, REPEATING, and REPEATING their own persuasive messages in language the general public understands.

Timing is crucial. You've got to know when to deliver messages, how to use the media, and how to build momentum so the campaign peaks on election day.

Because the factors that draw people to candidates are

THE BALLOT MEASURE

absent, voters are much more open to changing their minds over the course of a ballot measure campaign. People *often* like the concept of a measure, but don't like the specific provisions. Let's look at tracking poll results from the 1994 Arkansas campaign on the so-called "Safe Workplace Amendment" to illustrate the point.

From what you have heard about Amendment 6,
do you plan to vote for it or against it?

	Jan	July	Sept 7/8	Sept 25
Strongly FOR	16 \	17 \	13 \	18 \
Somewhat FOR	19 } 42	12 } 34	12 } 28	8 } 29
Lean FOR	7 /	5 /	3 /	3 /
Lean AGAINST	3 \	3 \	3 \	2 \
Somewhat AGAINST	6 } 12	4 } 14	10 } 33	9 } 37
Strongly AGAINST	3 /	7 /	20 /	26 /
Don't Know/Refused	48	51	39	34

Look what happened. Strong supporters held steady at about 17 percent over nine months. The shifts to our side came from every other group of voters: somewhat for, leaning for and the undecideds. (This same shift has occurred in nearly all the nineteen campaigns I've managed and won.) We were going to defeat Amendment 6 by a three-to-one margin when the Arkansas Supreme Court removed it and six other measures from the ballot just three weeks before the election.

You'll note the significant movement between the July and first September tracking polls. We went on the air with our media campaign in mid-August. We caused voters to change their minds on Amendment 6 by highlighting the fine print of the JOB KILLER in the media and campaign materials.

Here's one panel from a brochure that my good friends at Cranford/Johnson/Robinson/Woods of Little Rock produced for the campaign:

POWER IN THE PEOPLE

THE INITIATIVE THREATENS NEARLY EVERY ARKANSAN

Threat #1 is to Arkansas workers. A study requested by Arkansas Insurance Commissioner Lee Douglass concluded this proposal would put 60,000 to 80,000 Arkansas jobs at risk. That's why it's called A JOB KILLER!

Threat #2 is to small businesses. This same study said the proposal would increase costs of workers' compensation by 75% to 100%. For small businesses, increases could be up to 400% – forcing many of them to shut down!

Threat #3 is to small family farmers. This proposal would bankrupt many small farmers in our state because – for the first time – they wouldn't be exempt from workers' compensation and would be forced to pay these enormous costs.

Threat #4 is to churches. Churches, too, would lose their exemptions. If this proposal is passed by voters in November, even churches could be sued for workers' compensation claims.

Threat #5 is to the workers' compensation system. This proposal would turn the workers' comp system into a partisan, political nightmare, run by elected commissioners making more than $90,000 a year.

Threat #6 is to taxpayers. Dr. Charles E. Venus, former professor of economics, University of Arkansas, has concluded this proposal would cost taxpayers $72 million in increased workers' compensation costs for cities, counties and school districts.

THE BALLOT MEASURE

The conventional wisdom is that there's a drop-off of voters from candidates to ballot measures. Don't believe it! People respond to ballot measures when they feel frightened or angry and when campaigns for the measures are organized. In the 1990 attempt to ban all abortions in Oregon, as many people voted against Measure 8, the ban, as voted for governor. In the 1991 pro-choice campaign in Washington state, one county where church members organized and used their power had 15,000 more votes against the pro-choice measure than any other issue on the ballot.

For measures on a November ballot, we don't usually begin active public efforts until late August or early September—much to the annoyance of activists. I can't count how many people have told me that I didn't know what I was doing because our campaign wasn't on television in March. But voters don't pay attention to ballot measures until weeks or days before an election. There are a few instances when early media has some merit: to educate the public on the issue so they will be able to understand and accept campaign messages that will follow; to attack the opposition's credibility or when you're facing a big budget opposition. But typically, to try to get voters' attention earlier would be a terrible waste of resources. Anyway, it isn't an issue with the citizen campaigns I've managed because we never had the money to start so early: More than 60 percent of contributions come in the last six to eight weeks of campaigns.

The time from January to mid-August isn't wasted. While our efforts are low-profile, we're working very hard and intensely organizing. If you look back at the chart on Arkansas tracking results, the movement through July was a result of this hard work. When we do go public, we frame the issue, have persuasive messages, and have a list of powerful, credentialed supporters and a broad-based grassroots committee in place. Our opponents never recover.

POWER IN THE PEOPLE

"YES" Versus "NO" Vote Campaigns

There are very distinct differences between campaigns in support of an issue and those against an issue. Determining these differences and implementing a strategy based on them makes the difference between winning and losing campaigns.

In developing a NO effort, we work to convince the public that the proposed solution is not acceptable, no matter how serious voters believe the problem is. Punching holes in the "solution" on several different levels, and building a coalition and spokespersons who oppose the issue on each of these levels, makes a strong NO statement. Generally, those against an issue, even if they don't agree on a solution, will join together to urge others to "Just say NO!"

On the other hand, it is far more difficult to win a YES campaign. First, you have to convince people there's a problem; then you have to convince them that your ballot measure is the solution. Unless the language of the measure is carefully written and popular among voters, supporters can easily be put on the defensive by a well-organized, diverse coalition working against the measure.

This general problem with a YES effort is worsened if the vast majority of the public doesn't know about or doesn't understand an issue. Most often, they'll say NO to issues they don't understand. It's a "If-it-isn't-broken, don't-fix-it," vote.

It's always important to deliver clear, concise messages on either side of an issue. Without them, however, you *cannot* win a YES campaign. In a YES campaign, you must know the size of your opposition and their possible messages before they swamp your effort with, "There may be a problem, but this proposal won't solve it," approach. If the NOs are first on the air with advertising and frame the issue that way, the YESes won't have a chance.

There are, of course, exceptions. The 1988 California initiative qualified by citizen health-oriented organizations, like the

THE BALLOT MEASURE

Cancer Society and the Lung Association, was out spent thirty-one to one by the tobacco industry. The citizens won.

Nationally, the NO side of major ballot measure campaigns wins at least twice as often as the YES side. That happens for two main reasons.

1. A NO is normally a vote for the status quo—and most people are comfortable with that. In fact, there are between 15 and 20 percent of voters who vote NO on every measure.
2. When there's confusion or doubt about an issue, voters vote NO.

If you're thinking about putting a YES measure on the ballot, think and plan very carefully! They're tough to win.

BALLOT LANGUAGE

It isn't possible to stress enough the importance of effective ballot language—the few words voters see on their ballots. Here's the ballot language on the pro-choice campaign in Washington state:

Shall state abortion laws be revised, including declaring a woman's right to choose physician-performed abortion prior to fetal viability?

Would you think that if you wanted to vote for abortion rights, you'd vote YES? In fact, after hearing the ballot language, 24 percent of those who said they would vote NO thought they were voting for a woman's right to choose. The media strategy and resources had to be spent telling voters they needed to vote YES to support choice.

To overcome this huge handicap meant our inadequate funds were spent clearing up confusion rather than convincing people to vote YES. We won anyway—but just barely:

YES Votes - 756,812
NO Votes - 752,590

POWER IN THE PEOPLE

The proponents who worked with the Attorney General's office to approve the wording are very good in their own fields but they clearly didn't know how to get good ballot language. This same group named their initiative THE REPRODUCTIVE PRIVACY ACT. When we asked voters in our first poll what they thought that meant, 79 percent DIDN'T KNOW! But we were stuck with the name.

If you want any chance of winning a YES campaign, then seek advice from experts—lawyers and political consultants—with proven success in drafting ballot language. And use polling to make sure you're solving the public's problem, not just your own.

If you're working to defeat a ballot measure, you'll need the advice of experts, too. There may be reasons to challenge the wording in court.

SIGNATURE GATHERING

To put a measure on the ballot, you have to get enough signatures to qualify it. Check with your City Clerk or Secretary of State to find out:

1. How many signatures you need?
2. How much time you have to collect those signatures?
3. What are the requirements for witnesses to signing?
4. What is the process for verifying the signatures?

Be sure to follow the rules carefully.
Don't give your opponents reasons for legal challenges—
They take focus, energy, time and money away from your goal.

Your organization may have enough volunteers to get the signatures you need or you may have to combine volunteers with paid signature gatherers. You'll want to use a variety of methods—gathering in high-pedestrian traffic areas like malls, signing parties, mail, coupons in a newspaper ad—to get your signatures. Whatever combination of methods you use, follow the rule of

THE BALLOT MEASURE

Lee Albright, of National Petition Management, who has a perfect record in qualifying ballot measures throughout the nation: Be sure to get 50 percent more signatures than you need; some will be disqualified.

Speaking of malls, some owners claim political activities are a nuisance to shoppers and they try to ban petition gathering. The law is quite murky and varies from state to state. Check with your Secretary of State's office to find out what the accepted practice is in your state. If you are working in malls, you may be able to avoid problems by being present but not pushy. If you have problems, don't create a scene. Get legal help at once!

I worked with the Oregon Medical Association a couple of years ago when they were circulating petitions to put an initiative on the ballot that would have added a twenty-five cent tax on every package of cigarettes. The taxes would have provided health insurance for 450,000 Oregonians who can't afford it. On page 190 is the eye-catching sign Brian Gard designed for doctors' offices so patients would ask doctors' receptionists about the sign. These discussions led to a discussion of the initiative and to be sure each signature was personally witnessed as required by Oregon law.

CAMPAIGNING IN LOCAL AND STATEWIDE ELECTIONS

Local elections are easier for grassroots efforts than statewide elections. Voters feel more connected with their local community, so they're more inclined to volunteer and contribute. There are fewer voters to persuade, so local elections are far less expensive. Traditional grassroots activities—precinct work, neighborhood coffees, get-out-the-vote efforts—are easier to organize and effective in reaching voters.

In statewide campaigns on controversial issues, it's television that wins elections. We defeated the ban on abortions in Oregon with 68 percent of the vote. We defeated it in every single county; The lowest vote in any county was 55 percent. We won

POWER IN THE PEOPLE

Help us help.

Ask how your signature can help Oregonians get the health care they need.

Authorized by Oregonians for Health Care, 5210 SW Corbett Ave., Portland, OR 97201, 1-800-842-4957

THE BALLOT MEASURE

with very emotional, powerful television spots produced by two of the nation's best, David Mitchell and Kim Haddow, of Greer Margolis Mitchell & Associates of Washington, D.C.

Grassroots organizers insist that walking precincts in highly controversial statewide ballot measure campaigns is vital to winning. Pollster Ernie Paicolopos of Opinion Dynamics wrote what my experiences have taught me: In high-turnout elections, grassroots organizational efforts are of little value. My colleague, Frank Schubert, says, "On ballot measures, undecided voters move like a tidal wave."

Tracking poll results for the 1990 NO on Measure 10 campaign in Oregon showed that from July, 1989 to mid October, 1990, NO votes increased only 3 percent, from 25 percent to 28 percent. Television advertising started on October 16, 1990. By October 27, the NO vote climbed to 34 percent. It reached 44 percent on November 1, and peaked at 52 percent on election day, November 6, 1990.

This measure would have required a teenage girl between fifteen and eighteen years of age to tell a parent before she could have an abortion—a position supported nationally and in Oregon in 1989 and most of 1990 by 75 percent of the public.

This testimony for television advertising in no way detracts from the superb support the campaign received from national organizations for a last weekend blitz and election day activities. But without the major television campaign, we could not and would not have won!

Look at it another way. In Washington state, voter turnout at the 1991 off-year election was 1.5 million, or 68 percent of registered voters; there was a 77 percent turnout in the 1988 presidential election. To win, we needed to convince more than three-quarters of a million people to vote YES. Imagine the share of our $1.2 million budget it would have taken to reach enough voters to make a difference with door-to-door literature drops, mailing, or telephoning. With that money, voters could be

POWER IN THE PEOPLE

bombarded with powerful, persuasive television. If door-to-door marketing were effective on a large scale, then car dealers and soap makers—with their huge resources—would market door to door. They don't. They use their resources effectively with television.

Of course, it's necessary to have speakers available to respond to civic organizations and media interviews and to have brochures and bumper stickers for people who want to pass them out. But if you want to win BIG, then you need to buy as much television as your budget allows. And if your budget requires you to pick between grassroots activities and television, go with television. That's how you move voters in large enough numbers to cause a tidal wave.

Conventional Strategies May Be out the Window

Absentee balloting and vote-only-by-mail—or mail-vote—elections are throwing conventional strategies out the window.

Local elections where a low voter turnout is expected can be won or lost on absentee ballots. So can major, high voter turnout statewide elections. The outcome of the 1991 pro-choice campaign I managed in Washington wasn't known until over 200,000 absentee ballots were counted. We won the election by a 4,222 out of a total of 1.5 million. But we won!

In the last several candidate campaign seasons, it has become common practice for candidates to send absentee ballots to their supporters. It helps to get their voters to vote. (Voters used to need a reason for voting absentee; that's not true anymore.) But in 1996 for the first time, a United States senator was elected by a mail-vote election: The vote was for Packwood's replacement. In the special primary, ballots were mailed between November 15 and 17 and had to be received by county election offices no later than 8 P.M., December 5. Ballots for the special general election to fill the seat were mailed on about January 14 and had to be received by county election offices no later than January 30.

The fourteen-year history of voting by mail in the Portland

THE BALLOT MEASURE

area shows that about 50 percent of ballots are returned within three days after voters receive them and peak two or three weeks before election day. Political consultants know that the increasing use of absentee ballots and vote-by-mail elections will make huge differences in overall campaign strategies, message development, and media placement.

The two reasons given by Oregon Secretary of State Phil Keisling for holding mail-vote elections are to increase voter turnout and reduce election costs. As proof of his reasons, the May 1995 state and local mail-vote elections had a turnout of 44 percent; the May 1994 primary election was 38 percent; 1995 costs were $1.24 a ballot, 1994 were $4.33. Even adding the thirty-two cents voters pay for postage, they still save! Supporters of the mail-vote concept also believe it will decrease the amount of negative campaigning.

Opponents think vote-by-mail will make elections more a contest of strategies than an exchange of ideas. Others believe that these new techniques, rather than opening up the democratic process, will simply create a lot more work for consultants.

To the argument that mail-voting leads to massive voter fraud, proponents point out that every signature is visually checked against each voter's original signature—something that doesn't happen at the polls.

Only time will tell which predictions and arguments are right.

BENEFITS OF WINNING

When you win a ballot measure campaign, the benefits last beyond election day:
1. You and your group gain increased prestige as winners who know how to get things done.
2. You can turn the victory into good membership building and fund-raising opportunities.
3. A BIG, BIG win discourages your opponents from future ballot measure attempts and legislative efforts.

Here's to your BIG, BIG win!

PART V

PEOPLE-POWER SUCCESSES
And How These People Won

I know no safe depository of the ultimate powers of society but the people themselves.

Thomas Jefferson

As we've talked through organizing, building public support, getting action, and the ballot measure process, we've talked about dozens of people-power successes. There are common threads woven through all those powerful stories. Like Alice Paul, the successful people believed "Nothing is impossible." They had patience, tenacity, paid attention to details, and pushed their minds outside mental boxes so they found new possibilities and different solutions. They are all people of vision.

Our nation is changed forever because of magnificent courage of people with dreams of freedom. Paul Revere. Alice Paul. Rosa Parks. Martin Luther King, Jr.

Our cities and towns are changed forever by the visionary volunteers who used their people power to leave us a heritage. City parks. Libraries. Schools and universities. Trees. Hospice

POWER IN THE PEOPLE

programs. Clean rivers. Public art and museums. Hospitals. Transportation systems. Community gardens. Street lights.

Let's look at stories of a few people of our own time who may not be mentioned in history books but, by successfully using their people power, have been pioneers and dreamers in their own unique ways.

20

PEOPLE-POWER SUCCESSES

Ralph and Charlene Bauer, Huntington Beach, California

Long-time political activist, Ralph Bauer and his wife Charlene, have refined the art of community organizing since I first met them in 1965. The Bauers were always in positions of leadership—elected, appointed, or informal—when the influx of outsiders turned Huntington Beach, with 30,000 people and square miles of bean and strawberry fields, upside down.

Thirty years later, because the Bauers and other newcomers were visionaries, nearly 200,000 residents enjoy good schools, a city-wide park system, a major library designed by internationally known architect, Richard Neutra, the 1,200 acre Bolsa Chica wetlands, and a new, $3,000,000 art center. A clean, sandy beach fronts the entire city. It is the longest, continuous stretch of beach in any city in California—saved by citizens from wall-to-wall apartment and condominium developments.

Now retired from his career as international marketing manager for Unocal, Bauer, a Ph.D. chemist from UCLA, dedicates every hour of every day to making Huntington Beach an even better place to live. Bauer attributes his success to turning

POWER IN THE PEOPLE

the dreams and visions for his city to realistic action plans. These plans evolved through consensus building by a broad spectrum of citizens who had desire but initially lacked leadership and direction.

As a regular monitor at Huntington Beach City Council meetings, Bauer found a growing constituency of residents dissatisfied about a number of unresolved neighborhood and city issues: the need for a stop sign, deteriorating water quality, dislocation of a mobile home park, preservation of wetlands, excessive housing densities, proposed destruction of one community to clear the way for a bridge to the next city. Bauer felt the city was divided into isolated communities, each struggling alone to move the Council into action that reflected the needs and concerns of its neighborhood.

Beginning in 1991 at each Council meeting for over a year, Bauer made a list of the people and organizations who testified and noted the issues that concerned them. To begin building a city-wide coalition, he sent targeted letters directed to the specific concern of each neighborhood. From that list he created the Committee of 400—a group that mobilizes into action around the unresolved problems that brought them together. They write letters to the Council and local newspapers, lobby, recruit neighbors and friends to join in the action—and most important, THEY VOTE!

In addition to its issue-related work, the Committee of 400 works for the election of candidates. Joined by active homeowners' and civic associations, this core campaign committee did door-to-door precinct work and got out the vote, an effort that earned Bauer, the top vote getter in a field of twenty-two candidates, a four-year-term on the City Council.

Bauer emphasizes that raising campaign funds from everyone in the community is critical. The Committee of 400 has held many fund-raising events: among them one at twenty dollars per ticket; another at one hundred dollars. Fund-raising costs with a range of ticket prices allows everyone in the community the

PEOPLE-POWER SUCCESSES

opportunity to play an important part of the "dreams-to-reality" movement.

But the most successful fund-raising is done by Bauer in one-on-one phone calls. It isn't unusual for him to make over 1,000 calls during a campaign. Like Betty Roberts, Bauer is successful because he has credibility, is highly respected, works hard, and isn't afraid of rejection. Bauer asks for what he wants—and most often gets it.

The commitment of citizens like the Bauers working for practical city planning, recreational activities and cultural programs has created a city for others to use as a model. Huntington Beach was recently named America's safest, large city and the number one city for business development in California.

The people of Huntington Beach are lucky to have Ralph and Charlene Bauer working with them!

Elaine Cogan, Portland, Oregon

The citizen involvement program that Elaine Cogan, a partner in the planning and communications consulting firm of Cogan, Owens, Cogan, designed for the City of Portland's strategic planning process earned an Outstanding Achievement award from the U.S. Conference of Mayors. She got her leadership training in the League of Women Voters.

In one of her recent victories, Cogan helped organize citizens and small business owners save their "industrial sanctuary" from the invasion of a major warehouse store where many people in the community say they love to shop. The City of Portland created the sanctuary several decades ago to attract stable employers to an area of high unemployment. The City also provided incentives to businesses that agreed to stay in the area and pay good family-level wages.

The warehouse store owners saw the sanctuary's cheap land and good freeway access as the ideal place to locate another giant market. Given the political climate and encouraging economic

POWER IN THE PEOPLE

developments of all kinds, the warehouse store's advisors said they couldn't lose. Sanctuary supporters said the warehouse store would ruin their industrial environment and encroach on the neighborhood. They won round one when the City Planning Commission favored their arguments. Still, the warehouse store management was advised they couldn't lose if they appealed to the City Council, an elected body more likely to be "pro development."

Enter Cogan.

She framed the issue as the "people versus big business." In a three-month campaign, she and others mobilized people and small business owners, collaborated with land use attorneys, planners, and public relations specialists, and organized a campaign to defend the Planning Commission ruling to the City Council.

Foolishly, the warehouse store played right into their hands. In six, full-page ads and special mailings to hundreds of its members in the Portland area, the store tried to paint the people's campaign as "anti-business." Huge mail bags of letters were delivered to the City Council members who trashed them without opening them because of their obvious bias.

To counter the big spending, Cogan put a human face on the campaign. At the Council meeting, the warehouse store's case was given by button-down-collar corporate types who cited the value in terms of dollars the store would bring to the city. Speaking for the people and from their hearts, were small business owners and managers and people from the neighborhood. Offering a solution, some testimony suggested other available and more appropriate sites.

Cogan credits the testimony of a divorced, single mother who now earns a living driving a forklift for a company in the area; she spoke to the hearts of Council members. Before her job in the "sanctuary," this mother testified, she was on welfare and used food stamps. She noted that the warehouse store doesn't take food stamps.

PEOPLE-POWER SUCCESSES

After listening intently through nearly ten hours of testimony, the Council voted five to zero for the people. The people won—as they nearly always do when issues are framed as "not anti-business, but pro-people."

Cogan says, "It was a sweet victory!"

Denis Hayes, Seattle, Washington

On April 22. 1995, in communities across the nation millions of Americans joined Denis Hayes, Executive Director of Earth Day 1970, to celebrate the twenty-fifth anniversary of the start of what some people call the most successful social movement in our nation's history. As a result of the public awareness that the first Earth Day started building, nearly 80 percent of Americans now call themselves environmentalists. Thanks to the people power that first Earth Day activated, we breathe cleaner air, drink purer water, and have cleaned up contaminated land. Recycling has become a way of life for communities, government agencies and private businesses.

This great social movement began when then-Senator Gaylord Nelson (D-WI) asked twenty-five-year-old Denis Hayes, a graduate of Stanford's law school, to assemble a staff and stage an Earth Day. The organizers used one of their generation's favorite techniques, "teach-ins," to activate students across the nation.

Their success was unbelievable. Estimates are that twenty million people in the United States and Canada took part in rallies. Hayes recalls, "I started the day with a sunrise ceremony for 10,000 in front of the Lincoln Memorial, then flew to New York and addressed maybe a half million people on Fifth Avenue, then to Chicago for a giant rally at the foot of the Calder statue, back to Washington for a huge rally at the Washington Monument, and then on to the late-night talk shows. There were so many rallies in the major cities, and the crowds were so spectacular—much bigger than we had expected or planned—that we knew we had unleashed a political tiger."

POWER IN THE PEOPLE

"The huge success of the first Earth Day lay in the way it reached out to everyone with a simple, clear message," Denis Hayes writes. "And it helped to fashion a majoritarian consensus around environmental values that still endures." That was proven in 1990, when an estimated 200 million particpants in 141 countries took part in the twentieth anniversary events.

Hayes is now working to broaden awareness of environmental sensitivity to corporations. "Companies that behave responsibly and manufacture environmentally attractive products will have a very substantial advantage in the marketplace of the (1990s) next millenium. They will reduce their production costs by saving energy; reduce their legal liabilities by avoiding toxics and inspire their workers with a vision of a sustainable future. Green companies are going to eat their competitors' lunch."

Here's to you, Denis Hayes, for setting the standard for the best in coalition building and for making the earth a better place to live!

Barbara Irvine, Moorestown, New Jersey

Barbara Irvine's commitment to adding the Equal Rights Amendment to the United States Constitution drew her away from her second-in-command position at the State of New Jersey Division on Women. With degrees in chemistry and counseling, Irvine took a position that required experience in four fields she admittedly "knew nothing about": historic preservation, fundraising, coalition building, and media relations.

My first contact with Barbara Irvine was when she wrote me in the fall of 1986 at the suggestion of our mutual friend, Amelia Fry, Alice Paul's biographer. Irvine was President of the Board of Trustees of the Alice Paul Memorial Fund. Her letter of October 31, 1986, came on letterhead listing the twenty-eight HONORARY COMMITTEE members, including former First Ladies Rosalynn Carter and Betty Ford, the Governor of New Jersey, members of Congress, Gloria Steinem, actress Marlo

PEOPLE-POWER SUCCESSES

Thomas, and actor Alan Alda.

"The Estate of Alice Paul, a prominent suffragist and author of the Equal Rights Amendment, will be sold at public auction on November 15, 1986 . . . included is the desk of Susan B. Anthony, memorabilia from the suffrage era, and exhaustive records of Miss Paul's work for women's equality around the world," the letter announced.

These national treasures are now at the Smithsonian and Radcliffe College thanks to Irvine's leadership in organizing a national fund-raising effort for the Alice Paul Centennial Foundation, in conjunction with the Smithsonian Institution's National Museum of American History and the Arthur and Elizabeth Schlesinger Library on the History of Women in America at Radcliffe College.

Soon after that victory, Irvine took on the challenge of getting Paulsdale listed on both the New Jersey and National Registers of Historic Places, with the ultimate goal of having the property designated to the more exclusive and prestigious National Historic Landmark list by the National Park Service. In her research Irvine discovered that, although women sparked the historic preservation movement, less than 5 percent of all National Historic Landmarks honor women or their contributions. Irvine's coalition building skills and media relations brought victory again. Paulsdale was named to the prestigious list in 1991.

In early 1988, Irvine received word that Paulsdale, Alice Paul's birthplace, would be put up for sale. The property, "an oasis in the middle of encroaching subdivisions," sits on six and one-half acres of land. The owners, understanding the historic importance of the 175-year-old, twelve-room, Greek Revival farmhouse, offered the property to the Paul Centennial Foundation for $465,000, about half its true market value.

Using her creativity and "just do it" attitude, Irvine organized a consortium of seven banks who agreed to loan $365,000 for the purchase of Paulsdale. She got the New Jersey Economic

POWER IN THE PEOPLE

Development Authority to guarantee that loan. The property owner carried a $50,000 second mortgage. An anonymous "friend" loaned an additional $25,000. Fund-raising from individuals raised the remaining $25,000 needed. *The New York Times* headline, February 1, 1990: Suffragist's Birthplace Is Bought. Within two years, both the second mortgage and the "friend's" loan were repaid; the $290,000 loan balance remaining in November 1995 will be paid off in the next three years.

Major funding for the "Preserving Paulsdale" project was received from Arronson Foundation, Campbell Soup Company, Levine Foundation, Bear Stearns and Company, New Jersey Public Service Electric and Gas Company, Knight Foundation, Tomlinson Family Foundation, and Orleans Corporation.

"Preserving Paulsdale" was widely reported by media, including *The New York Times*, *USA Today*, *The Philadelphia Inquirer*, the Associated Press, and Nation Public Radio.

Some accomplishments for someone who admittedly didn't know anything about historic preservation, fund raising, coalition building, or media relations! Irvine's next dream is to make Paulsdale an educational center to address the challenges facing American women and their families.

Barbara Irvine is truly the "Apostle for Paulsdale!"

The Susan G. Komen Breast Cancer Foundation, Dallas, Texas

"With a few hundred dollars of her own and a shoe box full of friends' names," Nancy Brinker founded the Susan G. Komen Breast Cancer Foundation to honor her sister who died of the disease in 1982. Since then, breast cancer has gone from "being the unspeakable to the beatable."

The Foundation is "a national advocate" for breast cancer issues. Each year hundreds of thousands of women receive the life-saving message of early detection through Komen outreach efforts. Early detection would reduce by 30 percent the 44,000 women who will die of breast cancer this year, according to the

PEOPLE-POWER SUCCESSES

American Cancer Society.

Together in partnership with the federal government, the Foundation provides funding for breast cancer research, life-saving screening in innovative mammogram vans, and treatment programs. Other partnership efforts include important education for individual citizens and government officials.

The Foundation has established a national toll-free breast care help line (1-800-I'M AWARE), where trained volunteers answer questions, offer helpful information, and give moral support to breast cancer patients and others.

By the end of 1995, the Foundation raised more than thirty-nine million dollars. Some of the funds come from the Foundation's "Race for the Cure," a five-kilometer event held in sixty-six cities in thirty-five states and the District of Columbia. In 1995, 250,000 concerned and committed people participated in the events.

Nancy Brinker and the Komen Foundation make the list of People-Power Successes because, through their effective education programs, legislation requires health-insurance companies to cover routine mammograms for women over thirty-five years of age in more than forty states! The Foundation's education campaign has also led to passage of legislation that requires informed-decision options for breast cancer patients in eight states.

Many women live because of the wonderful works of Nancy Brinker and the Komen Foundation.

Stacy Brewer Pittman, Little Rock, Arkansas

Stacy Brewer Pittman, public and media relations consultant, used her professional expertise and personal energy to turn tragedy into an on-going, lives-saving triumph. In 1987, this mother of three-week-old Allyson became a widow. She was twenty-seven years old. Her husband, Tim Brewer, newly named partner for one of Little Rock's largest law firms, was killed by a drunk driver in a head-on collision. Pittman's success story was

POWER IN THE PEOPLE

featured in *Family Circle's* "Women Who Make a Difference."

Struggling with depression after her husband's death, Pittman finally realized she had to do something positive in his honor. She started doing what all good media people do: gathering facts. She learned that 68 percent of highway fatalities in Arkansas were alcohol-related—nearly 20 percent above the national average. She learned that Finland has one of the highest rates of alcoholism in Europe, but one of the lowest rates of alcohol-related driving fatalities. And she learned, while attending a conference in that country, about its designated driver program.

With encouragement from her father, Bob Sells, Pittman used another of her talents: She formed a diverse coalition of community leaders, organizations and concerned individuals who could help solve the state's drunk-driving problem. Supporting organizations include the Arkansas Alcoholic Beverage Control Board, the Arkansas State Highway and Transportation Department, the Arkansas Chapter of the Public Relations Society of America, the Arkansas City Attorney's Association, the Arkansas Hospitality Association (representing hotels, restaurants and bars), the Arkansas Press Association, and the Arkansas Game and Fish Commission.

One subcommittee selected the slogan: "Be a Highway Hero—Drive a Drinker Home." The kick-off campaign was a statewide event of simultaneous media announcements on the steps of over fifty county courthouses in Arkansas.

Highway Hero education programs encourage responsible use of alcohol. Alcohol Server Training has taught over 1,200 waiters/waitresses/bar and hotel managers in the state to serve alcohol responsibility. The Mocktail Contest taught bartenders methods to discourage patrons from drinking too much—and not to drive if they did. The contest's first place prize for the best non-alcoholic drink was an all-expenses-paid trip to Miami, Florida, provided by American Airlines. Harbor Hero, a designated driver program on land and water, stresses no drinking by

PEOPLE-POWER SUCCESSES

boat drivers. The Spring Fling Campaign, funded by the Beer Institute of America, established driver public information programs on college campuses throughout Arkansas. High School Hero, a teen-teaching program, is being developed.

The four-year-old Holiday Highway Hero Campaign, praised by the state's law enforcement community, has virtually eliminated drunk driving fatalities in central Arkansas during December. Participating cab companies report a record increase in requests to drive people home.

Advocates provide different kinds of support. The Arkansas City Attorney's Association recruited legal and law enforcement personnel to lead local committees. The Arkansas Hospitality Association distributes Highway Hero brochures, buttons and bumper stickers to its members. The National Highway Traffic Safety Administration provided start-up money for Alcohol Server Training. The Arkansas Press Association helped get advertising and editorial space with a public relations value of $30,000 at a cost of only $8,000 by encouraging papers to donate advertising and editorial space. Members of the Public Relations Society of Arkansas created and produced for free all publicity.

Since its beginning in 1989, the Highway Hero Campaign has built great public awareness of the dangers and tragedies of drunk driving at the same time the campaign stresses personal responsibility. As a result, Arkansas has dropped from fourth in the nation in drunk-driving fatalities to eighteenth. And for four consecutive years there have been zero alcohol-related fatalities during December in central Arkansas.

What a tribute to Tim Brewer by Stacy Brewer Pittman!

Michael Reid, Portland, Oregon

We've talked a lot about getting a stop sign. Michael Reid didn't get that, but he worked the political system so the streets in his neighborhood are safer. His inspiration came during a trip

POWER IN THE PEOPLE

to Yellowstone National Park. When he asked why the "pocked and potted roads worn down by overuse and neglect" weren't repaired, the ranger replied that every time they were fixed more animals and tourists were victims.

Reid saw the parallel between the roads in Yellowstone and his own neighborhood: You make good roads, you get dead children. "That's how I see it." Working for three years to get "traffic calming" tools installed in his northeast Portland, Oregon, neighborhood, Reid wanted safe streets for children, so he and his neighbors could sit on their front porches and visit without the annoyance of noisy cars speeding by at above forty miles an hour in the residential area that had a posted speed limit of twenty-five miles an hour.

The NE 21st and NE 24th Avenues Neighborhood Traffic Management projects were introduced at an Alameda Community Association meeting in January 1993. Interested neighbors saw a slide show of traffic control options and heard an outline about the neighbor involvement process. A couple of months later, the volunteer group met with Portland's traffic department to hear feedback on potential solutions. A year later, another meeting was held so neighbors could comment on proposed solutions.

In the July 1994 Association Newsletter, Reid noted that neighbors were calling about traffic problems on other streets. He advised them to contact the right person or office and then added this caution: "Don't expect an immediate response; keep calm and take notes about who and when you called. The point is, action happens in City Hall when many people call about a problem. You really are the only one who can start the action!"

In September 1994, neighbors voted on the proposed solutions: speed bumps and curb extensions. Many neighbors spoke at the meeting. Impacted residents were sent mail-in ballots. With about half of the people responding, the vote was four to one in favor of the proposal, and the City Council approved it.

In his Newsletter column, Reid wrote, "Thank you to those

PEOPLE-POWER SUCCESSES

who worked on the project. Thanks also to those who opposed it as your comments were valuable in spotting problems."

Reid has done a lot of "empowerment" over the years. He says it takes time and people, good communication, and "ownership" of the program. When consulting to "top down" types about empowerment, Reid counsels that the first actions should be ones where the answer can be either yes or no. He believes that many non-empowered people just want "to say NO! long and hard" before they get to working on community action.

With his dramatic image of dead children, Reid finally had his success. Now, the children, their families, the neighborhood and Reid himself are all safer and happier. Congratulations, Michael Reid, for a great example of "defining the issue"!

The People, Business and Political Leaders, Portland, Oregon

Thanks to the courtesy of *The Oregonian*, on the next page is a reprint of their July 19, 1995, editorial told better than I possibly could:

POWER IN THE PEOPLE

WEDNESDAY, JULY 19, 1995

Restoring self-confidence

When tough planning decisions prompt self-doubts, outsiders' accolades can restore sense of purpose, poise

It takes planning, not just luck, to keep a metropolitan region livable. A June 16 article in The Charlotte Observer newspaper serves to remind us of that.

For three days in June, 89 members of the Charlotte Chamber of Commerce's 40th Annual Intercity Visit team explored Portland. MAX impressed them. So did the retail and residential development along the downtown waterfront. They described Pioneer Courthouse Square as "a people magnet . . . in the heart of downtown." They regarded the Trail Blazers' new Rose Garden sports arena as a testimonial to public-private cooperation. They liked the city's "bustling nightlife."

But what did they learn?

"They attribute much of Portland's progress to good planning — including regional transportation planning — and excellent consensus-building among government, business and citizens," wrote Doug Smith of the newspaper's staff.

"The lesson here is that total community involvement was sought and seems to be the binding force that makes their programs work," said Charlotte-Mecklenburg school board member George Battle.

"Organized neighborhood associations have been vital to the successful development of Portland and its high quality of life," wrote Mohammed Jenathian, a tourism industry executive.

"In Portland they have vision," wrote Darrell Williams, a county commissioner, "and the city, along with the private sector, is willing to finance that vision. . . . We cannot even pass school bonds."

The visitors clearly were struck by Portlanders' ability to make tough decisions and envious of it. They expressed a need to develop that capacity, but they acknowledged how difficult that might be.

☐

To plan is to decide, and that indeed can be difficult and scary.

Hundred-million-dollar choices to build light rail and to bank undeveloped land for parks and recreation can create decision overload: Do we know what we're doing? What if we're wrong? What are the consequences? Why not let nature take its course?

If self-doubt leads to a community's decision-paralysis, individual choices make up the region's "face" largely unchecked, and regional development loses the imprint of collective choice.

Making collective decisions forces residents to become literate and engaged. They tend to become supportive, however a particular tussle turns out. Consensus building is community-building. It is an antidote to an uninformed, alienated, isolated and angry citizenry.

Building a base of public opinion takes time. It often is painfully slow. But patient talk here ultimately produces action — action that cities around the nation envy.

That still doesn't make it easy, but the accolades tell us that our doubts should haunt us less.

PART VI

CONCLUSION

And so we've come to the end of our visit. We've shared a lot of ideas as we've talked about organizing for action, building public support, getting action, ballot measure campaigns, and people-power successes. We've talked about some of life's profound lessons. You've heard some of my life's story—the fears, sadnesses, learning experiences, and successes. Woven all through our time together you've even met some of the most important people in my personal and professional world.

This time with you has been a wonderful learning and creative experience filled with discovery for me. I've been stunned at how hard the process has been; talking about things I do every day is much easier than putting the words on paper. It's been an all-consuming effort. I haven't read the paper or magazines or books for months without searching for an idea or a quote to make a point. Experiences long forgotten have brought other gifts of examples to give you. Ideas popped in my head in the shower. I was awakened from a deep sleep with the solution for an edit I was struggling with. A fortune cookie broke one mental block. The unexpected death of Betty Robert's husband and my friend,

POWER IN THE PEOPLE

Keith Skelton, got me past another block. And there have been delightful serendipitous surprises.

Just last week as I was writing the conclusion to *Power IN the People*, a new friend, Blake Wilson, reminded me of Dr. Seuss's people-power parable, *Horton Hears a Who!* You remember the story. The gentle, whimsical elephant, Horton, heard the voice of a tiny person yelling for help. Rescuing the tiny person perched on a speck of dust, Horton put the speck on a clover blossom. The beasts of the jungle heaped poor Horton with ridicule. But being a kind spirit, he persevered. Then he discovered he'd saved not just one tiny person but a whole town of tiny people and their buildings. They were all perched on that speck of dust. A mean eagle snatched the clover blossom and carried it far away.

After hours of searching, an exhausted Horton finally found his tiny people only to be captured by a gang of beasts. He pleaded with the town mayor, "Make yourselves heard. *So come on, now, and TRY!*" The tiny people made a racket with their instruments—a tom-tom, tin kettles, brass pans, garbage pail tops, old cranberry cans, and all kinds of horns. But to no avail. The mean animals simply couldn't hear the tiny people. At last, the mayor found the "shirker," a "young twerp."

> "This," cried the Mayor, "is your town's darkest hour!
> The time for all Whos who have blood that is red
> To come to the aid of their country!" he said.
> "We've GOT to make noises in greater amounts!
> So, open your mouth, lad! For every voice counts!"

The shirker yelled and the elephant smiled. 'Do you see what I mean? . . . They've proved they *are* persons, no matter how small. And their whole world was saved by the Smallest of All!'"

I end this time with you filled with great hope because of very special young people in my life who make political action and involvement in their communities part of their everyday

CONCLUSION

lives. Brian, the fifteen-year-old neighbor who watches my cats and home when I travel, visited yesterday and talked about the lessons he's learned during his in-depth study of our nation's Constitution. Bill, my son-in-law, whose passion for wetlands preservation has led to innovative negotiations assisting rice growers in Texas to provide landing places for migrating geese. My first born, Christine, who makes a difference as a junior high teacher of Texas history. My second born, Carrie, who helped clean up south central Los Angeles after the riots following the Rodney King verdict.

And I'm hopeful, too, that from this time we've shared you'll have gained the expertise and confidence to want to do more than you've ever done to make our precious democracy work better. Will you join an organization so your voice is added to others on an issue you care about? Study a new issue so you're well informed when you talk to others about it? Write letters to the editor of your local paper or a national magazine? Make a commitment to contribute to political issues and candidates you believe in? Lobby? Testify at public hearings? Run for office or seek an appointment to a board or commission?

I'm looking forward to hearing from you. I'd like to know where you found solid ground and when you soared. Let me know how you've used your power.

Were there things you've learned from our visit that helped you? How?

Were there things that didn't work? Why not?

And please tell me about your people-power successes!

Just send a note, some of the materials you've produced or clippings about action you've taken to me at:

Jeanette Lona Fruen
P.O. Box 19265
Portland, OR 97280-0265

POWER IN THE PEOPLE

Thank you so much for your gracious hospitality, the coffee and cookies were delicious! How did you know Russian teacakes are my favorites?